Is Happiness a Cigar Called Hamlet?

by
Sujit Bhattacharjee

Grosvenor House
Publishing Limited

All rights reserved
Copyright © Sujit Bhattacharjee, 2020

The right of Sujit Bhattacharjee to be identified as the author of this
work has been asserted in accordance with Section 78
of the Copyright, Designs and Patents Act 1988

The book cover is copyright to Sujit Bhattacharjee

This book is published by
Grosvenor House Publishing Ltd
Link House
140 The Broadway, Tolworth, Surrey, KT6 7HT.
www.grosvenorhousepublishing.co.uk

This book is sold subject to the conditions that it shall not, by way of
trade or otherwise, be lent, resold, hired out or otherwise circulated
without the author's or publisher's prior consent in any form of binding or
cover other than that in which it is published and
without a similar condition including this condition being imposed
on the subsequent purchaser.

A CIP record for this book
is available from the British Library

ISBN 978-1-83975-043-4

ACKNOWLEDGEMENTS

There are many people who encouraged me to set down my thoughts concerning the topic of happiness in the form of this book, or who paved the way to bring it to fruition.

I would particularly like to thank my son Abhik and daughter Suparna for their unfailing support and encouragement.

As always, my brother Sudip, sisters (Purnima and Sumita), together with my brother-in-law Sibesh were sources of immense inspiration.

I am extremely grateful to Dr Andy Cope for taking the trouble to read my manuscript and offering his supportive comments.

I would like to thank all those at Grosvenor House Publishing (GHP) who helped with the publication of this book, particularly Becky Banning for her invaluable assistance. I also greatly appreciate the guidance and advice of Darin Jewell on promotional matters.

Finally, I am so indebted to my wife Gourie for her many valuable contributions to this book and also to every other aspect of my life. She is and has always been the foundation on which my happiness is built.

Unless otherwise stated, the views and conclusions expressed in this book are my own and any errors are entirely my responsibility.

CONTENTS

1	Introduction	1
2	Meaning of Happiness	4
3	Happiness History	7
4	Happiness in Different Religions	13
5	Positive Psychology and *The World Book of Happiness*	23
6	Cynics of Happiness	26
7	Growth Fetish – Money Does Not Buy Happiness	29
8	Government and Happiness	33
9	Happiness in the UK	37
10	Happiness in America	43
11	Happiness in India	47
12	Happiness in Schools and Colleges	52
13	Happiness in Films	57
14	Social Media and Happiness	62
15	Ways to Be Happy	66
16	Conclusion	79
17	References	89

1

INTRODUCTION

Happiness is a subject that concerns everyone. Yet, finding happiness in life is not easy. Many books have been written, thousands of articles published and substantial research undertaken about what happiness is and how to achieve it. The subject has preoccupied the minds of numerous religious leaders, philosophers and thinkers, from ancient to modern times.

During the last three decades, there has been a huge surge of interest in this subject. This is largely because of the growing popularity of the role of positive psychology in academia to treat happiness as a subjective appreciation of life. The focus is on the strengths and virtues that enable individuals to take control of their lives. This has led to various fascinating practical forms of exploring human wellbeing, such as yoga, exercise and meditation to help people to become happier. Further, in parallel to this development, a vast happiness industry has sprung up, particularly in America, to guide the lives of ordinary human beings towards the coveted land of happiness.

I am conscious of the fact that I am just a tiny wave in a vast sea of hundreds of different people who are more knowledgeable on the subject of happiness.

However, no one can truly claim to have found and popularised a single key to happiness for all the people. Many different routes have been suggested from time to time but no single route is followed by all or works for everyone.

My book is an attempt to:

- outline the meaning and history of some of the concepts of happiness
- summarise some of the major spiritual and non-spiritual thoughts and paths suggested for living a happy life
- try to explain the emerging influence of positive psychology on the subject of happiness, with America and the UK as epicentres for the happiness industry
- draw attention to a few films which convey some useful messages on the subject of happiness
- discuss the similarities and differences in the British, American and Indian pursuits of happiness
- attempt to analyse various academic studies, past and present, concerning happiness, and, finally
- provide my own personal reflection and understanding of what happiness is and the way to live a joyful life.

I hope that my book, however amateurish it may seem, will still be a useful addition to the wealth of material that is already available in the field of happiness.

My book is a short one. The importance of the subject and the growing number of valuable studies carried out on it, probably suggest that a more detailed and longer book was required. However, I decided to emulate the newly emerging trend in writing, which is more in praise of short books than long ones.

2

MEANING OF HAPPINESS

In the 60s and 70s, the TV advert *Happiness is a Cigar Called Hamlet* was in the public consciousness for a long time. It was a long running popular campaign for Hamlet cigars which featured in television, radio and cinema commercials; and on bill boards. The underlying message was that, lighting and smoking the cigar helps a man forget and overcome an awkward situation he finds himself in. I was a smoker at that point, so the advert was quite appealing to me, with the kind of pleasure I used to get from smoking. I have referenced this advert in the title of my book because I find it both funny and thought-provoking. It draws attention to the serious subject of human happiness by exaggerating the benefits of lighting and smoking a particular brand of cigar. "Think like wise men but communicate in the language of the people," the Irish poet William Butler Yeats said about what makes a good advert.

A more recent advert I found attractive was a display placard in the O2 Arena in London: 'Happiness is watching Roger'. I love tennis, I play tennis and Roger Federer has always been immensely joyful for me to watch. There are many other adverts which appeal to viewer's emotions but the critics say these trivialise the concept of happiness. However, one cannot deny that they are popular, stick in your mind and can give a pleasing sense of relaxation; although the feeling may last for some fleeting moments only.

Everyone has a different idea of happiness. This is the reason why there is no agreed definition of it. In the real world, people seek happiness in various ways.

Seeking material comforts is one common way. Eating good food, indulging in luxuries, falling in love, seeing your children being born and grow are some other well-trodden paths. Closely related to happiness is the addictive type of pleasure which is associated with drugs, greed, gambling etc. In general, these are considered mundane pleasures and defined as hedonistic in nature. The commonality present in all is that these physical or emotional feelings are normally related to various material objects, events or occurrences, which themselves do not last and, therefore, the kind of pleasures that arise out of them are generally of short duration.

There are many kinds of happiness, achievable through gradual refinement of the mind.

A longer-term path to finding happiness is where a person seeks to elevate mundane pleasures to a higher realm. This can be achieved by leading an 'engaged life' through interesting sustained activities, including devotion to art, culture, sport, music etc. However, in this realm, one still remains self-centred; not paying attention to the world outside. Those at this level are viewed as being generally satisfied with the state of their own wellbeing.

Higher than this level is the holistic one, in which a person finds satisfaction in all aspects of existence by leading a meaningful and ethical life devoted to societal needs. This is a more permanent, deep and transcendental type of happiness described in various aesthetic and spiritual forms in different cultures and religions.

In 2015, Eric Greitens, an American politician, author and former naval officer, wrote a book entitled *Resilience: Hard-Won Wisdom for Living a Better Life*. This was based on the lessons he learnt from Iraq and Afghanistan wars and his knowledge of the teachings of both ancient and modern thinkers. In this book, he has classified three major forms of happiness in a simple way but very much in line with the aforementioned classification of short- and long-lasting forms of happiness:

- the happiness of pleasure, which is sensory
- the happiness of grace, meaning love and gratitude, and
- the happiness of excellence, which is the pursuit of something greater and meaningful in life.

Happiness, therefore, can be defined as a mental state of wellbeing, ranging from sensual pleasures to non-sensual contentment and, finally, to intense joy.

There are thinkers, like the English philosopher Jeremy Bentham, who have sought to define happiness in terms of the enjoyment of pleasure and the avoidance of pain. This is considered a natural and rational aim of human life. So, a happy life is one that maximises feelings of pleasure and minimises pain. However, the measurement of pleasure and pain is a difficult task in itself. It is even more difficult to formulate the criteria by which to evaluate them. Bentham himself acknowledged this.

3

HAPPINESS HISTORY

Although it is hard to find a common definition of happiness, the concept itself has a rich and meaningful history. Philosophers and thinkers through the ages have valuable advice about how to be happy. In this respect, it is worth outlining a range of valuable contributions from some well-known thinkers and scholars, from the eminent Chinese philosopher and thinker Confucius, to Martin Seligman, commonly known as the founder of positive psychology.

CONFUCIUS (551 BC to 479 BC)

According to the influential Chinese philosopher Confucius, ordinary human beings have the power to transform themselves to noble persons (the Junzi) by pursuing the idea of 'jen'. This is righteousness and concern for the wellbeing of others. In order to be happy, one should acquire virtuous qualities such as benevolence, love, honesty and kindness and foster family values and intimate ties with society.

SOCRATES (470 BC to 399 BC)

The first known person in the West to espouse the idea that happiness is obtainable through human effort was

Socrates. According to him, happiness is what everyone desires, and it is obtainable specifically by controlling and harmonising physical and external desires and cultivating virtue and self knowledge. Such efforts produce one's deepest good – a divine-like tranquillity of mind – which is real happiness.

ARISTOTLE (384 BC to 322 BC)

One of Aristotle's most influential works is the *Nicomachean Ethics* where he said that happiness is the ultimate purpose of human existence. Pleasure, wealth, status, friends and other goods have value only in giving a temporary state of pleasure. They are a means towards achieving the ultimate 'good', which is desirable in itself – and that is happiness.

Aristotle also believed that "He is happy who lives in accordance with complete virtue." By 'complete virtue', he meant a good moral character for the enrichment of human nature. As man has a rational capacity that is different from other animals, the way to reach enrichment is to act in accordance with virtue and exercise of reason.

ZHUANGZI (369 BC to 286 BC)

The Chinese philosopher Zhuangzi drew a clear distinction between two kinds of happiness.

The first kind is one of fleeting joy, where people seek more and more of wealth or fame, or physical comfort, and become unhappy if they cannot get more.

The second is more permanent in nature and mentioned in his book *Supreme Happiness* as 'Dao'; a mysterious semi-spiritual power which is present in our natural surroundings.

There is no need to tamper with this power, because 'Dao' always brings benefits to human beings. So, to Zhuangzi, happiness is nothing but 'Wuwei', which is not doing anything i.e. not a contrived action but going along with the way of things.

Whereas Confucius emphasised the importance of social relationships and Aristotle the role of reason, Zhuangzi refused to let reason dominate lives. Instead, he put faith in the mysterious power of 'Dao' (sometimes called 'Tao') as the source of our happiness. In this respect, he was a precursor of the modern concept of 'flow' made popular by the Hungarian psychologist Mihaly Csikszentmihalyi. Flow is a highly enjoyable state of being immersed in a task, like playing music or reading a good book. This helps people to be more creative and happy.

STOICISM (3rd century BC)

Three famous thinkers who helped to found and popularise Stoicism, an ancient school of Hellenistic philosophy, were Zeno of Citium, Lucius Seneca, and Epictetus. Being stoic is being calm and living in harmony with nature, of which we are all a part. This implies that the universe is a rationally structured system and that the one who is content with his fate, without wishing for what he has not got, is a wise man. Stoicism provided a compelling answer to the question "what do I want out of life?" by asserting that the greatest blessing of mankind is within us and that enduring happiness and the tranquillity of mind come from being a rational and virtuous person.

ABU HAMID AL-GHAZALI (1058-1111 AD)

A foremost authority on Islamic theology, Al-Ghazali wrote extensively on the topic of happiness. In his *Alchemy of Happiness*, he said that ultimate bliss could not be found in any physical thing, or passions or desires, but was achievable in discovering through reason, imagination and experience of one's identity with the Ultimate Reality. Only the prophets have attained such identity and become truly happy people. Ordinary human beings are happy to the degree to which they can emulate the spiritual paths of the prophets.

THOMAS ACQUINAS (1225 to 1274)

According to the Italian priest and philosopher Thomas Aquinas, one of the towering figures in Western theology, the perfect happiness (beatitude) is obtainable only in the afterlife by those who achieve a direct perception of God by the exercise of reason and the contemplation of truth and virtue. This puts Aquinas midway between those like Aristotle, who believed complete happiness was possible in this lifetime, and someone like the Christian thinker St. Augustine, who taught that happiness, consists merely in the anticipation of the heavenly afterlife.

JOHN LOCKE (1632-1704)

John Locke, a major English philosopher, coined the phrase 'pursuit of happiness' in his book *An Essay Concerning Human Understanding*. His writings influenced Voltaire and Rousseau and paved the way for the French and Americana revolutions. Locke's theory of rights was incorporated into the famous statement of people's inalienable rights to 'life, liberty, and the pursuit of happiness' in the American Declaration of Independence.

Locke made a distinction between 'imaginary happiness', associated with pleasure, property, or the satisfaction of desire, which only gives temporary gratification, and 'true happiness', which is intense and long-lasting. Locke has called true happiness 'solid' as it reflects the overall quality of life.

MARTIN SELIGMAN (born 1942)

In modern times, Martin Seligman, an American psychologist, is considered a pioneer of positive psychology. According to his findings, the most satisfied, upbeat people are those who have discovered and exploited their unique combination of 'signature strengths', such as humanity, temperance and persistence. They provide contentment with the past, happiness in the present and hope for the future.

According to him, happiness has three dimensions – the Pleasant Life, the Good Life and the Meaningful Life.

The Pleasant Life constitutes such basic pleasures as companionship, the natural environment and our bodily needs.

The next level is Good Life, which is achieved through employing our unique virtues and strengths.

The final stage is the Meaningful Life, in which a deep sense of fulfilment is reached, using our virtues and strengths for a purpose greater than ourselves.

The views offered by Socrates, Aristotle and the Stoics are what are called 'eudaemonia' or 'eudemonia', or 'makarios' in Greek or 'beatitude' in Latin, meaning 'real blessedness'. The Greek word 'endaimonia' has the prefix 'eu' which means good and the part 'daimon' means spirit, thus implying that happiness is a matter of soul. The last bit, 'ia', implies a lasting and permanent state. In contrast, the English word 'happiness' implies subjective satisfaction or contentment. Happiness, in the modern view, as advocated by Martin Seligman, is a subjective appreciation of life – by identifying and cultivating our unique strengths, every day.

4

HAPPINESS IN DIFFERENT RELIGIONS

The holistic form of happiness has been the objective of many religions through centuries. To explore this further, one needs to look at what the different religions offer regarding their ideas of happiness.

CHRISTIANITY

In Christianity, the word 'happiness' is rarely mentioned in the Holy Scriptures. There is no mention of it in the *New Testament*. The scriptures use another term, 'joy', as an equivalent to happiness. The scriptures contain many other synonyms: 'happy', 'blessed', 'pleasure', 'delight,' 'contentment', 'glad' and 'rejoicing' are some examples.

In Christian religion, true happiness is not some shallow euphoric state of mind. It is a state of blessedness arising out of a deep relationship with God. The submission to God's teachings is paramount to finding the sense in life. The Bible makes it clear that, the less you are concerned about your happiness and the more you are concerned about Him (God), the happier you become. Furthermore, to be happy eternally, one needs to act virtuously. Ethical behaviour during life is important to bring happiness in this life as well as salvation after death.

"Thou dost show me the path of life; in thy presence there is fullness of joy, in thy right hand is pleasures for evermore" (Psalm 16:1).

JUDAISM

The great classicist Rabbi Nachman famously said, "It is a great mitzvah to be happy always," because there is no greater way to bond with God than by experiencing happiness in one's relationship with Him. However, there is no precise equivalent to the word 'happiness' in Hebrew. Three important words to describe happiness are:

- Simcha (happiness in general)
- Osher (lasting happiness)
- Ditza (sublime joy).

Happiness is not considered the ultimate goal; joy ('simcha') is more crucial in life.

There is acknowledgement, in Judaism, that seeking one's own pleasure can never result in long-lasting happiness. The one who lives unselfishly will bring joy to others and get the reward of a rich, spiritual life.

"The Holy Spirit rests on one who has a joyous heart" (Jerusalem Talmud - Sukkah).

HINDUISM

In Hinduism, happiness is an end which all human beings should aim for. What Hinduism calls happiness ('sukha') and its opposite, misery ('duhkha'), are relative experiences called 'dualities' and we must rise above them to discover real happiness.

Hinduism recognises gradual stages or degrees of happiness, depending upon the level of one's spiritual awareness. Happiness pervades this world. It can be found from so-called worldly temporary happiness to everlasting spiritual bliss through union with Ultimate Reality (Blissful Self or 'Atman'). This has been explained in the *Vedas* through four aims in human life:

- material wellbeing (artha)
- duty (karma)
- righteousness (dharma), and
- ultimate happiness (moksho).

This means that the happiness that we get in our day to day life is only a shadow and is elementary. The real happiness is inherent in us and is much deeper and wider as pure bliss.

"He who is unattached to the external world and its objects and is attached to the inner self, will attain supreme happiness, which is everlasting" (Bhagavad Gita 5.21).

ISLAM

Islam sees the path of happiness ethically. As human beings, we desire the inner peace of heart and enrichment of the soul. This enrichment, in Islam, comes through not possessing wealth but through 'Submission to Allah Almighty'. As the eminent scholar Islam Bukhari said, "True enrichment does not come through possessing a lot of wealth, but true enrichment is the enrichment of the soul."

In Islam, meaningful activities result in enrichment of the soul. This requires spreading the inner peace to the family, the community, the society and the world at large. So, Islam strongly advises us to maintain family ties, keep strong social relations and help others, as necessary steps to achieve happiness.

"Those who believe, and work righteousness, their Lord will guide them because of their faith, beneath them will flow rivers in gardens of bliss" (Qur'an 10.9).

BUDDHISM

In Buddhism, the word 'happiness' is derived from "piti" in the early Pali texts, which means deep tranquillity (nirvana).

The Buddha who was referred to as the 'Happy One' said that happiness is not to be found in the outer social world but in a transformation of mind that generates wisdom. What prevents us from experiencing happiness is suffering ('dukkha') that each and every one of us undergoes. The more self-centred we become, the less happy we are. Achieving freedom from suffering and attaining peace of mind has always been the ultimate goal of Buddhism.

Peace of mind or equanimity will result only through regular practice of pure thought and action, by following an eightfold path of:

- Right Understanding
- Right Thought
- Right Speech

- Right Action
- Right Livelihood
- Right Effort
- Right Mindfulness and
- Right Concentration.

"From Joy there is some bliss, from Perfect Joy yet more. From the Joy of cessation comes a passionless state and the Joy of sahaja (the innate) is finality" (Hevaira Tantra).

JAINISM

Happiness, in Jainism, is about freedom from pain and can be achieved by leading a life of simplicity and non-attachment. That is the message of 'aparigraha' (virtue of non-possessiveness), not to allow greed for material goods to dominate our thoughts and actions, because this will lead to attachment and pain.

Like the Hindus, Jains believe that karma is what determines the quality of life. The happiness of one's present life is the result of his or her actions – good and evil – in the previous life.

"The self that has developed equanimity, if endowed with pure activities, attains heavenly happiness (Acharaya Kundlund, Pravachansara).

SIKHISM

Sukhmani, (The Pearl of Happiness) is a fundamental text of faith in Sikhism and has described different kinds of happiness and pleasure. This text and the Holy text *Guru Granth Sahib* have expanded this further by referring to two types of individuals among us. Those who always think of themselves (Muhnmukhs) and those who always think of the Lord (Gurmukh). The former suffer from pain forever, the latter are always wonderfully joyful. When a man worships God, he attains eternal bliss by cultivating all the good qualities of love and devotion.

Similar to Hinduism and Jainism, an important belief in Sikh religion is karma, one's action in life. The consequences of it decide whether a soul can be joyful or not.

"Guru tells us that the meek and humble win God's love, while the haughty and the vain find no peace or joy" (Sukhmani).

The need to have a joyous life has been stressed by many other religions and sects.

BAHA'I FAITH

The followers of Baha teachings believe that in order to achieve true and lasting happiness, we must fill our hearts with the love of God.

This will lead us to the love of humanity and eventually to the door of tranquillity and spiritual happiness. That is how one will find a real purpose in life and true happiness. The physical comfort from wealth, success and status is short-lived. Spiritual happiness is eternal.

Three principles are central to the Baha'i idea of true happiness:

- the unity of God
- the unity of religion, and
- the unity of humanity.

"Human happiness is founded upon spiritual behaviour" (Abdu'l Baha).

ZOROASTRINISM

Zoroastrianism believes that Ahura Mazda (Wise Lord) is the source of all goodness and happiness. Happiness lies in promoting harmony with everything he created and treating it with love and reverence. In Zoroastrian teachings, it is incumbent on every man and woman to live the life of right thoughts, right words and right deeds. Only in this way can they be happy and acquire the wisdom of 'Vohu Mana', the good mind.

"Doing good to others is not a duty. It is a joy, for it increases your own health and happiness" (Hymns of Zoroaster).

TAOISM

Tao means 'the way' or 'the path' and is an ancient Chinese philosophy. Taoists, whose ultimate goal is wisdom, do not believe that a rich material life or high social status will bring real happiness. They emphasise the idea of living a simple and balanced life in harmony with the natural order underlying the activity of the universe. One important principle to navigate life and find happiness is to go with the flow of the natural state of things. This is the reason why Taoism is also referred to as Daoism.

"Man follows the earth. Earth follows the heaven.
Heaven follows the Tao. Tao follows what is natural" (Scripture Tao te Ching xxv).

SHINTO

Rituals rather than a belief are at the core of Shinto; the reason why it is not strictly considered a religion, but an important aspect of Japanese day to day life.

The rituals enable human beings to communicate with some invisible spiritual forces of nature and powers called 'kami', manifested in mountains, rivers and trees. The Japanese Shinto followers believe that human beings are basically good but need protection. So, for a happy life, these spirits must be prayed to and placated to achieve harmony in all aspects of human life. Shinto ceremonies ('matsuri') are designed to appeal to the kami for benevolent treatment and protection.

"To be fully alive is to have an aesthetic perception of life because a major part of the world's goodness lies in its often unspeakable beauty" (Yukitaka Yamamoto).

TENRIKYO (TENRIISM)

The worldly aim of Tenrikyo, a new Japanese religion, is to teach and promote a joyous life through charity and abstaining from greed, selfishness, hatred, anger and arrogance. These are considered 'dust' that should be swept away from the mind by voluntary actions (efforts) and mindfulness called 'hinokishin'.

Tenrikyo followers firmly believe that a joyous life is the original intended state of mankind and emphasise that charity towards others is the way to find joy in oneself.

"I created you human beings because I desired to see you lead a joyous life" (Tenrikya Ofudesaki 14.25).

PRIMAL (INDIGENOUS) RELIGIONS

The popular perception of most primal religions in Africa, Australia (Aborigines), Polynesia (Maoris) and North America (Indians) is that they are ritualistic, sacrificial and superstitious. However, most primal societies are considered to be happy ones. The World Happiness Report in 2017 ranked the Africans as one of the happiest and optimistic people in the world, in spite of poverty, illness and conflicts in many parts of the country. The reason is that while happiness is sought universally, its meaning and implications differ widely, particularly with regards to the Africans, Aborigines, Maoris and North American Indians.

Further, religion and faith play vital roles in the lives of people in primal societies because of their emphasis on happiness as a 'collective concept' and not an 'individualistic' one. This has helped to create a very strong social structure in primal societies around which people are taught to venerate ancestors, live in harmony with nature and worship the power found of the spirit that resides in all things in the universe.

In African primal societies, the belief is strong that morality lies in veneration of the ancestors and in conforming to age-old tradition. The Aborigines in Australia have apparently no religion but maintain a deep affinity with the spirit in the natural world. There are no temples, as such, in Maori cultures but there is deep faith in the life force and they have strong spiritual bonds with the land and ocean. Relationships with the spirit, animals and earth are vital for the happy life of the North American Indians.

Christianity and Islam have made great inroads into most of the primal religions but tradition lives on regardless. Life can, indeed, be joyful without an obsession with material happiness.

History shows that religions, although largely dictated by scriptures, faiths and traditions, were effective in promoting wellbeing in societies at different times. Furthermore, some useful research carried out on links between religion and happiness indicates that religious people, in general, are happier. They tend to have more social contacts and support to overcome depression and other stressful situations that beset life so often.

This view has been challenged by the idea that the religiously-committed people are capable of causing more distress and sufferings to others. There is also the counter argument that there are countries like Denmark and the Netherlands which are less religiously affiliated but recognised as two of the happiest countries in the world.

Historically, through the passage of time, and with the upsurge in more secular forms of research on happiness, the focus gradually shifted from ancient religious forms of teaching to a scientific analysis of happiness in the shape of positive psychology. This examined how people actually experience their lives and sought to identify factors which positively foster a happy and meaningful existence.

5

POSITIVE PSYCHOLOGY AND *THE WORLD BOOK OF HAPPINESS*

The positive psychology movement or 'Happiness Studies', as it is often called, was started in 1998 by Doctor Martin Seligman. He reinvented the discipline of psychology from treating mental illness, as its primary objective, to making the lives of people more fulfilling by nurturing their inner strengths and qualities. Following the publication of his book *Authentic Happiness*, the focus shifted to individuals taking positive control of their own lives and disregarding external circumstances, with the belief that they make no significant difference to human happiness.

This new focus attracted many heads of government and religious leaders, including the former British Prime Minister David Cameron and His Holiness, the Dalai Lama.

In 2010, Leo Borman, a distinguished scholar on happiness from Belgium, published a collection of essays by happiness experts from 50 different countries. This book, *The World Book of Happiness*, attempts to explain what happiness in its various forms means to all of us. The book was sent by Herman Van Rompuy as

President of the European Council to more than 200 world leaders. This resulted in championing a national wellbeing index as an appropriate measure of overall human happiness for a country, in place of economic growth. This also echoed the view of Jigme Thinley, the Prime Minister of Bhutan, who initiated the much-valued Gross National Happiness measure in 2008 for his country.

The aforementioned book provides some interesting insights into the concept of happiness. To give a few examples:

"Comparison spoils your happiness" (Professor. Claudia Senik, University of Paris-Sorbonne)

"Income is important for happiness, but more and more income does not lead to more and more happiness" (Stavros A Drakopoulos, Professor of Economics, University of Athens)

"Happiness can and must be learned" (Professor Ernst Gehmacher, OECD)

"We are happier when we believe more strongly in our own abilities and efforts than fate and destiny" (Professor Paolo Verme, University of Turin)

"Humans are social animals. We are happier when we are connecting with other people" (Doctor David Watson, University of Iowa)

"Happiness is like a muscle that can be developed" (Miriam Akhtar, British Positive Psychologist)

"Concentrate on the 4 Fs of happiness: faith, form, family and friends" (Professor Yew-Kwang Ng, Monash University and Melbourne)

The underlying message in this book is a positive one-identify factors which foster or deter happiness in life and make recommendations which people can follow to tackle these factors in order to think better, perform better and make sound decisions.

While this positive psychology-oriented notion of happiness is a welcome development, there are critics who consider it naive to foster what they view as 'cultural compulsory happiness'. "Positive thinking has turned happiness into a duty and burden," said Danish philosopher Svend Brinkmann. Susan David, a Harvard University professor and psychologist, argued against repressing or apologising for our negative feelings. Our emotions, both positive and negative, make up what we are as human beings. By pushing negative feelings away, we choose not to learn about ourselves, and they are bound to come back magnified. These criticisms led Professor Edgar Cabanas and Eva Illouz, authors of the book *Manufacturing Happy Citizens*, to accuse positive psychologists of advancing a western ethnocentric creed of individualism.

Despite the aforementioned criticisms, positive psychology has become incredibly popular. What has been witnessed recently is a dramatic upsurge in self-help books, coaches, seminars, courses and lectures on fostering positive thinking. As a result, happiness has also rapidly become a marketable concept. A vast amount is now being spent in money-spinning self-improvement types of industries all over the world – particularly in the USA and this country.

6

CYNICS OF HAPPINESS

Not everyone believes that happiness is something either achievable or desirable.

There are pessimists, like the German philosopher Arthur Schopenhauer, who viewed happiness as gloomy, rare and temporary. According to him, "There is one inborn erroneous notion that we exist in order to be happy."

Friedrich Nietzsche, another German philosopher, considered the mere pursuit of happiness, defined as that which gives pleasure, 'a dull waste of human life'. Referring to the English philosophy of Utilitarianism and its focus on total happiness, he rejected happiness as something we desire above all else. To him, the idea of finding a meaningful life was the more desirable alternative.

There are some experts who argue that happiness is an inborn trait. So, urging a person to become happier is like insisting that he or she become taller. This may sound like an exaggeration but there is a general acceptance of the fact that there is a link between our genes and happiness, but it is complex and fragile. A positive psychology study by Sonja Lyubomirsky, Professor of Psychology at the University of California, emphasised that 50% of our emotions are controlled by our genes, 40% by behaviour and thoughts and 10% by our life experiences.

There are other experts who are of the view that happiness has, and still is, an elusive animal; difficult to track down. According to the American poet and philosopher Henry David Thoreau, "happiness is like a butterfly: the more you chase it, the more it will elude you". So, it appears, wanting to be happy is what can make people *un*happy. The advice from Thoreau is that if you can only turn your attention to other things, happiness will come gradually. The ancient Chinese philosopher Laozi (also known as Lao Tsu) expressed it in a slightly different way by saying, "Seek happiness not too greedily."

In the opinion of the English novelist Charles Snow, "the pursuit of happiness is a most ridiculous phrase: if you pursue happiness you will never find it." He also believed that it is the most natural thing in life to feel unhappy; because happiness alternates with unhappiness like day and night – the recognition of it avoids self-oriented stress and unhappiness.

The above cynicism led several more experts to say that there is more to life than happiness. The lives of many wonderful and successful people like Beethoven, Tchaikovsky, Van Gogh, Milton Proust and Dostoevsky are examples of people showing dedication for creativity at the cost of their health and wellbeing.

The American writer, Eric Wilson, in his book "*Against Happiness: In Praise of Melancholy*" deplored the idea that unhappiness is something to be ashamed of. To be unhappy is very often construed as an acknowledgement of being a failure, and this cannot be true. Without misery and failure, one cannot truly understand and appreciate joy.

Unfortunately, the commercial world, nowadays, is highly invested in the idea of happiness, telling a person that not only is happiness achievable, but that you are a failure if you do not attain it.

7

GROWTH FETISH – MONEY DOES NOT BUY HAPPINESS

If money can make us happy, all the rich people in this world would be more than happy with their lives. On the other hand, all the poor people would be thoroughly distraught with their conditions. But they are not.

"Does money automatically bring wellbeing?" is not a new question – it has been asked through the ages.

Regarding our desire for wealth, Christ said, "Blessed are the poor in spirit." This is because it does not matter how much money you have, it will give you no satisfaction if those around you earn more.

Aristotle wrote, in the *Nicomachean Ethics*, "the life of money-making is one undertaken under compulsion, and wealth is evidently not the good we are seeking: for it is merely useful for the sake of something."

St Francis of Assisi, son of a wealthy silk merchant, rejected materialism in the form of worldly goods for happiness and opted for a life of poverty instead.

In 1974, the American economist Richard Easterlin published a significant study to demonstrate that increases in income do not result in a commensurate increase in subjective wellbeing. The study had its origin in the paradox that although the Americans, in general, were getting richer, they did not seem to be noticeably happier. He conceded that money makes some difference, when you have very little, but once you have a certain level of income, the euphoria of happiness wears off from any extra income.

The Australian Professor of Public Ethics, Clive Hamilton, in a provocative book *Growth Fetish*, talked about the same contradiction of modern politics. After many years of sustained economic growth, people were not any happier. According to him, 'growth fetishism' is what lies at the heart of our social ills and is leaving people depressed and miserable.

Gucci designer Tom Ford achieved an enormous amount of fame and fortune in his life as a creative director of Gucci but underwent an anti-materialistic conversion later in his life. He then made it his mission to speak out against society's unhealthy obsession with material goods, which results in many becoming mentally ill and unhappy. He was remorseful about helping to create a socially harmful material world and urged society to value the non-material aspects in life by asserting, "the things that make me happy are the people in my life."

Another important study by two economists, Eugenio Proto of Warwick University and Aldo Rustichini of Minnesota University, reinforced the Easterlin belief that when average income reaches a certain level, people are happiest, but beyond that, they are richer but less contented, due to an 'aspiration gap'. The gap is the difference between actual income and the income people would like to have, which turns out to be a moving target; particularly for rich people.

Subsequently, two economists, Guoqiang Tian of Texas A&M University and Liyan Yang, an economist at Cornell University, developed a mathematical model to show that having more money does not necessarily mean greater happiness. They used a formula explaining that up to a critical income, more money may enhance happiness, but beyond that, more income is unlikely to have any positive effect.

Not everyone shares this view. There are critics of the Easterlin belief who suggest that life satisfaction always increases with higher income. Several research works have been published recently to overturn the 'Easterlin Paradox'. In their opinion, for people who are struggling financially, more cash always makes a difference to the level of their satisfaction. This view was made popular later by a new study by Justin Wolfers and Betsey Stevenson, two economists from the University of Michigan, in 2008. Their finding was that not only is there a clear relationship between income and happiness, there is no evidence of a saturation point above which this correlation stops.

Michael Norton, a professor at Harvard Business School, carried out another study, believed to be the first of its kind, focusing exclusively on millionaires. His study revealed that wealthier millionaires are happier than those with lower levels of wealth. The rich feel much happier if they can earn two or three times more than they earned before. However, this study conceded that on a scale of happiness they developed, this form of increase would only lead to a 'modestly greater wellbeing'.

Jeffrey Winters, Political Science Professor at Northwestern University, Illinois, conducted a similar study, focusing on billionaires. Every billionaire he interviewed was extremely excited by each additional increment of money he made. This was illustrated amusingly in the popular TV sitcom *Only Fools and Horses*. Del Boy, after becoming a millionaire, says to his brother, Rodney, "This time next year, we'll be billionaires!" However, whether one is a millionaire or a billionaire, the British philosopher Bertrand Russell's oft quoted dictum will still apply: "Beggars do not envy millionaires, though of course they will envy other more successful beggars." So, the impact of money on the wellbeing of rich people will depend on how well they compare with the other rich people around them.

Despite the efforts by some economists to portray a positive pro-materialist scenario of happiness, the concept of the 'Easterlin Paradox' has continued to receive recognition in academic circles. Lord Richard Layard, the Director of the Centre for Economic Performances at the London School of Economics, who was at one time David Cameron's economic guru, carried forward Easterlin's work, by restating that money does make people happier once basic needs like food and shelter are met. His book *Happiness: Lessons from a New Science* emphasised the importance of non-income variables on aggregate happiness.

This debate regarding the link between wealth and happiness will no doubt continue, because we cannot really predict clearly what actually makes a human being happy. While one cannot deny the importance of material things in life, there are matters beyond boundaries of economics, such as work-leisure balance, social relationships and the love and affection of people, which have a far more direct bearing on our sense of being happy or unhappy. This aspect has been discussed in more detail in later chapters.

8

GOVERNMENT AND HAPPINESS

It is difficult enough to measure individual happiness, because it varies, depending on how people go about things, the circumstances they are in, their environment, family, work, friends etc. It is even more difficult to measure happiness across the country.

Recent happiness research is having a big impact on practical politics of governments, with the realisation that decades of economic growth have made no substantial impact on the welfare of their citizens. This is because economic policies are mostly driven by the idea of growth. Surveys show that such policies do not help to increase social happiness. As a result, even the economists who, at one time, championed growth, have started looking for alternative criteria.

Research work by two economists, Guoqiang Tian and Liyan Yang, about income growth and happiness, was mentioned in an earlier chapter. Their advice to governments was that they should use part of their income to improve non-material factors for promoting social happiness. Reference was also made to the state of Bhutan, which has developed a unique concept of happiness in the form of 'Gross National Happiness'. The essence of it lies in the state provision of free healthcare and education, and social progress in an environmentally sustainable manner. This started in the late 1980s, with a series of five-year plans prepared as composites of both material and non-material needs of people; the byword being 'Gross National Happiness' (GNH) and not 'Gross Domestic Product' (GDP); normally used as a measure of a country's economic wellbeing.

However, as Tshering Tobgay, the young and articulate Prime Minister of Bhutan has himself admitted, his country still has many problems in terms of poverty, economy and people's expectations – a long way from the Shangri-La image with which the Bhutan Government is very often portrayed.

The relationship between income and happiness has now become an objective for many other politicians, social scientists and think tanks. The New Economics Foundation (NEF) which ranked UK 13th out of 22 European levels of happiness published a report in November 2010 on how local government can make people happy by improving regional services with more sustainable environmental practices.

Ex-Prime Minister, David Cameron, made the pursuit of happiness his political vision, which in turn led to the launching of the Movement for Happiness; an organisation to increase happiness and reduce misery in all spheres of life. In his book *Happiness: Lessons from a New Science*, Professor Lord Richard Layard, the UK's leading happiness economist, whose thinking is founded on the Utilitarian philosophy of Jeremy Bentham, expressed his belief that government has a responsibility for the happiness in society. Tackling poverty, ill health, conflict etc. on the one hand and improving mental health services, encouraging parenting support and positive lifestyles in schools on the other, are some of his proposals to promote happiness.

The Happiness Research Institute in Denmark was set up in response to the current global move towards wellbeing rather than wealth as a measure of national growth. The UN passed a resolution in 2011, urging member nations to make happiness 'a fundamental human goal'. The OECD (Organisation for Economic Cooperation and Development) has made life satisfaction one of the indicators of progress.

There is a growing recognition of the fact that public policy needs to reframe and reorient our institutions towards wellbeing and happiness. David Cameron's former adviser, Steve Hilton, in his book *More Human*, has lamented the fact that governments the world over have lost touch with the people they are supposed to make happy. He went on to say that to restore faith in politics, there should be recognition of the fact that there are things like happiness, love, joy, good health and fulfilment which make life worth living.

Rachel Sylvester, writing for *The Times* newspaper, echoed this sentiment by referring to the big divide "between those who see the world in terms of the individual and the market and those who think it is about the citizen and the state."

Sylvester also referred to a new book by *The Times* columnist David Brooks, *The Social Animal*, which has become a best seller. According to Brooks, governments will only be successful if they recognise that the world is moving from an 'economo-centric era' to a 'socio-centric' one. The underlying message in his book is eloquent: 'Statecraft is ultimately "Soulcraft".' The rising GDP does not necessarily correlate with happiness. The important goals of government policy-makers should be to improve the non-monetary aspects for both individual and national welfare.

9

HAPPINESS IN THE UK

It is only in recent years that politicians have started recognising the importance of happiness for implementing public policies. The analysis of national mood in this country over the past 200 years provides conflicting views. One found that Britain was happier in the 1880s, when Queen Victoria was on the throne. The mood had sunk during the First and Second World Wars, improved in the early 50s because of the end of wartime rationing, but slumped again in the 70s, reaching a very low level in 1982 – the year of the Falkland conflict. However, the result of research from Warwick and Glasgow University and the Alan Turner Institute in London found that "we could be richer than our Victorian time but less cheerful, it seems."

In modern times, The Office for National Statistics was asked by the former Prime Minister, David Cameron to create a happiness index for the population, indicating General Wellbeing (GWB), alongside the Gross Domestic Product (GDP). The survey, carried out in 2010/11, showed that about 75% of the population rated their happiness level at 7 or more out of 10. Another ONS report found a moderate increase in the average happiness index of 7.56 in 2018/19, compared with 7.52 in the previous year. More recently, the Independent Resolution Foundation think tank reported that the levels of self-reported 'life satisfaction' have improved considerably over the past 40 years.

This view of national wellbeing is not widely shared and there are many critics. Compared with other developed countries, the index for Britain's national wellbeing was lower. Furthermore, despite some economic indicators like wages and household spending showing year-on-year increase, it was difficult to discern any noticeable rise in happiness.

However, David Cameron's initiative provided the necessary impetus for the launching of the Movement for Happiness, an organisation to increase happiness in all spheres of life, in 2010. The movement was the brainchild of three academics: Lord Layard, the UK's leading happiness economist, (mentioned earlier), Anthony Seldon, Master of Wellington College and Geoff Mulgan, former Head of Policy at 10 Downing Street, with the spiritual guru, the Dalai Lama, as patron.

The movement has its root in the stated objective of positive psychology: to build a happier and more caring society in the form of greater social engagements. The result was a ten-point plan (ten keys) formulated for individual happiness. These are:

- Giving (doing things for others)
- Relating (connecting with family, friends, neighbours)
- Exercising (being active in taking care of the body)
- Awareness (bringing mindfulness into your daily life)

- Trying out (continuing to learn new things)
- Direction (setting goals to look forward to)
- Resilience (finding ways to bounce back)
- Emotions (looking for what is good)
- Acceptance (being content with what you are)
- Meaning (being part of something bigger).

The plan appears to be an effort to combine hedonic, mundane, emotional feelings with Aristotle's idea of the eudemonic happiness of having a purpose in life.

The reality TV series *Rich House, Poor House,* shown on Channel 5 in 2017, was about an affluent family swapping homes with a poorer one for a week. One particular episode showed two families who were, apart from how much money they had, very much alike in many respects; both being compassionate and sharing values for family life. The message at the end of the episode was that happiness is about being satisfied with what you have and sharing it with the people you love, and not stressing oneself about the wealth that divides people in real life.

Subsequent to this programme, *The Times* commissioned an exclusive YouGov poll to find out how important money is to British people. A massive 89% considered happiness, not money, to be most important but there was a decent-sized minority believing the opposite.

While the pursuit of happiness is enshrined in the American Constitution, here in the UK, people are less comfortable with the 'happiness hyperbole'. An outward display of emotion is not part of the national stereotype. Instead, the usual response, such as, "Cheer up, it may never happen" is viewed by many happiness experts as more likely to boost general optimism in the long run than an obsessive search for happiness. Furthermore, on a positive note, a research has found that in spite of being reserved, Britons are, in general, of a sunnier disposition than the French, Italians and Belgians.

As in America, happiness as a self-help industry has become big business in the UK as well.

Two British entrepreneurs, Andy Puddicomb from Bristol and Michael Acton Smith from Marlow, inventors of mindfulness and meditation apps Headspace and Calm, have made inner peace a big business in the USA. Both have tens of millions of subscribers.

Freelance journalist Michael Odell visited Glastonbury village, which has become a mecca of spiritual nourishment. His account is an interesting guide to this newly emerging self-help market. Along with meditation and yoga, he found the place offering a number of rituals involving crystals (placing crystals in the middle of the forehead and listening to an instrument); a gong bath in a temple (submission to the sound of gongs and bells to establish contact with a spirit or deity); chakra balancing (the pressing of four chakras on the forehead, sternum, belly and feet) and listening to soundtracks of waterfalls and birdsongs – all intended to stimulate positive feelings in the minds of people seeking physical or mental wellbeing.

Two of the latest wellness crazes on offer from the Lake District are horse meditation and yoga with lemurs. In both cases, the followers are expected to make forehead connections with a horse or lemur and find calmness in their presence.

Two entrepreneurs, Billie Quinlan and Anna Hushlak, have recently launched a digital platform called Ferly to popularise the latest sexual wellness trend.

Born in Poland, Michael Serwa arrived in the UK in 2005 with no money but soon became Britain's best-paid life coach, charging up to £30,000 to mostly rich but unhappy clients. He does not follow any particular school of coaching. His website says, "*My aim is to provide every single one of my clients with the coaching experience parallel to the Michelin-starred restaurant dining experience........ I am my coaching style*" This may not sound very professional or convincing but it appears that Michael Serwa has been successful in transforming the lives of a great number of rich clients.

Yoga and meditation, practised properly, provide tools and the means to move forward on the path to tranquillity. However, the same cannot be said about many of the unusual forms of finding happiness I have mentioned above. They offer a quick and relatively 'easy fix' road to spirituality but whether they are sustainable, beneficial or truly make for a happy life in the long run is another question.

Some members of the British Royal Family have shown keen interest in eastern spirituality and meditation. Prince Charles and Camilla, and now Prince Harry and Meghan Markle, seem to be happily following that path. The Prince of Wales' charity funds yoga to help prisoners to develop their spiritual welfare. The Duchess of Cornwall has disclosed that she practises many deep breathing exercises. Kate, Duchess of Cambridge, has revealed a passion for the Japanese 'shinrinyoku' – forest bathing – spending time in greenery. Prince Harry was reported to have said that he meditates "every day" and was seen wearing an Oura ring – a sleep and exercise tracker.

The search for happiness is universal and the Royal Family's enlightening stance on mental and spiritual wellbeing recognises the positive association between spiritualism and happiness.

10

HAPPINESS IN AMERICA

Human beings have a natural impulse to pursue happiness. America takes things one step further and happiness is codified in the Declaration of Independence. However, a significant proportion of Americans – about two thirds – feel that they are not very happy.

The 2019 World Happiness Report shows that the US dropped to No. 19, from No. 18 in 2018 and No. 14 in 2017.

In the report, many reasons are given as to why the Americans are dissatisfied: addiction, particularly leading to drug overdose, the role of social media, obsessive interaction with electronic devices, depression, self-harm and other indicators of low psychological well-being. Also, American society seems to be reflecting the Easterlin paradox. The standard of living has improved and so should happiness – but it has not.

Many believe that as more and more Americans became less happy, history evolved in such a way that the American goal was transformed to what is called 'consumptive happiness'. As a result, private pursuit has replaced public good.

Further, this has given rise to a vast happiness industry worth $2 billion, predicted to rise to $2.08 billion by

2022. This consists of prescribed self-improvement services and products of various sorts, including anti-depressants, books, seminars and motivational speakers, as well as some non-traditional self-improvement practices, as in the UK.

In this private pursuit, once one achieves a certain level of happiness, the aim becomes to go to the next level and so on. These results in what the American novelist Nathaniel Hawthorne described as "a wild goose chase that is never attained."

An example of the consumptive type of happiness is the account, in *The Sunday Times*, of a British journalist based in the USA, Sanjiv Bhattacharya. He recounts his experience of attending a private, spiritually themed 'soul salon' in California to which only people of power were invited. The event centred on 'a song conversation', with everyone singing in chorus, followed by meditation, together with breathing exercises and positive affirmations. According to him, "It's a classic story – the rich discover that happiness cannot be bought, so they turn to religion for meaning... ordering spirituality off the shelf." However, there was no doubt in Bhattacharya's mind that the organisers sincerely believed that influential people singing together helped to build community feeling, similar to the annual event of Burning Man at Black Rock City. Interestingly, *The New York Times* dubbed the sing-along at private homes 'Burning Man in your living room'.

The Burning Man festival draws thousands of people to the Nevada desert, in which the participants, known as Burners, seek to share experience of self-reliance, self-expression, community cooperation, civic responsibility and many other utopian ideas. This started as an anti-consumerist protest movement against the alleged profit-oriented and status-driven capitalist world we live in.

The event was the brainchild of Larry Harvey, who came up with the idea in 1986, when, on impulse, he set fire to a man on a beach in San Francisco. This was repeated each year until it became too big and was moved to Black Rock Desert in 1990. Some of the biggest names in social media are now involved in this event, but the presence of an increasing number of popularity-seeking, ultra-rich, social media billionaires and Hollywood stars is said to be threatening to damage its reputation.

British writer, journalist and author Ruth Whippman has written a book, *The Pursuit of Happiness*, about her personal experience of America's happiness industry, which is both witty and insightful. According to her, self-help books, yoga, meditation etc. are popular in many countries around the world, but in America, these have a high-octane approach, with its own vocabulary of empowerment. What surprised her most, was that in spite of investing an enormous amount of money and efforts into popularising the self-absorbed and individualistic approach to deliver happiness, Americans were not truly becoming happier. Divorced from communal wellbeing, this was compounding rather than resolving the problem of isolation and depression in society.

In this respect, *Belong*, a book written by the former investment banker Radha Agarwal, comes across as particularly relevant to banishing loneliness in society. The book is designed to get rid of the fear of missing out ('FOMO') or the fear of being left out ('FOBLO') and replace it with the joy of missing out ('JOMO'). To put this into practice, Radha launched an organisation called Day Breaker to encourage younger people to stage alcohol free events, with dance and music only. Her early life was all about bars, booze and parties, but this changed after she met her husband Eli at the Burning Man festival. As a "community architect", she was inspired to form Day Breaker, along similar lines. At a time when loneliness and social isolation are two major problems associated with younger people, Radha Agarwal's book, no doubt, offers a useful way for young Americans to remain connected and feel less lonely.

Despite the unhappiness experienced by many Americans, the majority have remained hopeful and feel optimistic about raising levels of happiness. One of the biggest changes already noticed is how people feel about the importance of non-economic measures involving families, communities and faith, for measuring the state of their welfare.

Further, experience shows that the more aggressively one pursues happiness, the harder it can be to find. This is likely to have prompted John Gerzema, the CEO of Harris Poll (one of the longest running surveys of public opinion in the USA) to say, "We are not that happy, but perhaps that's OK. Optimism, but not necessarily happiness, seems to be part of the American psyche. Perhaps we wear it like a coat of arms."

11

HAPPINESS IN INDIA

Happiness in India is both a curious and confusing matter for many Westerners because of the way it is perceived and manifested in the West.

Jean Dreze and Nobel laureate Amartya Sen argue in their book, *An Uncertain Glory*, that India's much heralded economic growth counts for little when the country has failed to provide the poor with their most basic needs. In contrast, a specific group of people are living in luxury highlighting the gulf between the lives of the poor and the rich. The economy has been growing fast for a long time but with limited results in terms of social progress and general wellbeing. There appears to be political apathy in regard to addressing it. This finding has been vindicated by the fact that the World Happiness Report for 2019, which showed India dropping down to 140 from its 2018 ranking of 133. This reflects ongoing, deep-seated weaknesses in India's socio-economic fabric.

However, this ranking has its critics, who have expressed reservations on the findings of the World Happiness Report on three important grounds:

1) The criteria used to assess global happiness vary from year to year. In 2019, the focus was on six

key variables: GDP per capita, social support, life expectancy, freedom of choice, generosity and corruption. Freedom of choice and GDP, rightly or wrongly, are not highly prioritised values in India. This also explains the surprising placement of countries like Mexico, Brazil, Russia and China above India in the World Happiness Report.

2) The variables used in this report were mostly to ascertain the general wellbeing of a nation but not the comparative subjective feeling of the happiness of people in different countries. There was admission of the fact that there was a noticeable surge in negative factors such as stress, worry and sadness in many of the countries topping its happiness index.

3) Although India ranks low in the World Happiness indices of happiness, an IPSOS Global Poll of more than 18000 people in 24 countries in 2019 showed Indians to be generally happier than the indices suggest, with more positive than negative feelings about wellbeing. India was ranked 9th with 77% on the happiness index, among 28 countries ahead of Mexico, Brazil and Russia, as well as Sweden, Belgium, Italy and Spain. This calls into question the criteria used to assess the World Happiness ranking. There are many other factors beyond economic prosperity that make people happy.

For the majority of Indians, happiness is about their approach to life, of which 'karma' is an essential part. Karma reflects the universal principle of cause and effect, action and reaction. It means that the sum of a person's actions in this and previous states of existence is what decides their fate in future existences. Karma permeates his day to day life. What both supports and strengthens this principle are faith in God, being kind to others, a calm mind and not being obsessed with material wealth. This helps people to look at life from a different perspective.

In this respect, an article titled *Happiness in India* by three eminent psychologists, Professor Robert Biswas-Diener, Professor Louis Tay and Professor Ed Diener, is truly illuminating. They explored Indian happiness in the context of both 'inside out' (meaning the effect of culture) and 'outside-out' (meaning the effect of money/income etc.) on life satisfaction. The basis was a comparative study of homeless people living in Kolkata with those living in Oregon and California. The study found that homeless people in Kolkata were either mildly satisfied or significantly more satisfied with themselves than the Americans in Oregon. They identified the reasons as being inside-out social factors, like close family relationships and a relatively ambivalent attitude towards poverty, associated with the Indian concept of karma in contrast to the thoroughly individualistic cultures of the West.

Travelling around different parts of India, Diederik Mallien, a travel writer from Holland, found Indians either busy doing a range of tasks or sitting or standing in groups and having conversations. What struck Mallien was that they appeared relaxed and calm in whatever they were doing with their lives, as if they did not give much importance to the word 'happy', like most Westerners do.

Another travel writer, Mariellen Ward from Canada, took several trips to India to recover from a personal tragedy in her life. She said that she rediscovered the joy of living amidst the crowded, chaotic, hot and dusty street corners and supplemented this with her knowledge and practice of the essence of yoga and spirituality.

This can be construed as testimony of a country where happiness can be found in a laidback culture. But the problem is that this often leads to a life of complacency and induces people to accept living in poor conditions as something over which they do not have any control. This, in turn, exonerates the government from showing any serious inclination to take action to tackle poverty and inequality. As a result, the country remains largely non-egalitarian. Happiness is as much about calmness and composure in life as it is about the adoption of the hedonic experience of day to day pleasure and comfort. This means that the influence of external material conditions, so called 'outside-in' factors, for both individual and collective happiness, should be given priority in a country where, along with spiritualism, there is also a rich tradition of materialistic philosophy from ancient times.

In this connection, it is worth mentioning an interesting development in India to create a Ministry of Happiness to improve the lives of India's citizens. The idea, in the words of Prime Minister Narendra Modi, was to "put a smile on every face" in the manner of Bhutan's concept of Gross National Happiness. The proposal was to implement it in a particular state – Madhya Pradesh – with programmes of yoga, spirituality, meditation, the arts and religious lessons. However, it failed to take hold due to political reasons. This explains why many critics viewed this initiative with cynicism and did not believe that this was a serious attempt to address the real, deep-seated social problems. However, the advocates of the new Ministry of Happiness appear hopeful and they point to one important consideration in support of its efforts – India's own long-standing history as the originator of 'contemplative practices'.

12

HAPPINESS IN SCHOOLS AND COLLEGES

It is encouraging to note that 'happiness' is now being taught in schools in various countries.

In India, a new happiness curriculum has been introduced in schools in Delhi, with an emphasis on personal wellbeing rather than on simply achieving higher grades. This has originated from the experience that too much pressure is being placed on students nowadays to attain top results, leading to depression and suicide. Indian universities follow stringent entry criteria and the pressure on young people to attain top results is enormous.

The Delhi programme lets students spend a part of each day listening to moving stories and meditating. The stated objective is to 'deliver the best-of-the-best human beings in society, to the nation'. His Holiness, the Dalai Lama, who was an adviser to this new curriculum, said at its launch, "Modern education focuses on material values and has nothing to offer regarding inner peace. Only India has the ability to combine modern education with ancient knowledge."

Many other states in India are in the process of introducing similar curricula in their schools.

In the UK, happiness has become part of an experiment introduced in primary and secondary schools from 2004 called SEAL (The Social and Emotional Aspects of Learning). The scheme is aimed to help children aged 3-16 years to develop their personal and social skills, including emotional wellbeing. Evidence shows that the SEAL initiative has the potential to create an ethos and environment in which a range of benefits to children is promoted and facilitated with support from staff and parents.

A happiness service in schools has been launched by a wellbeing organisation called Brilliant Schools, with support from Doctor Andy Cope, a teacher and author who is referred to as the Doctor of Happiness. The service aims to provide students with the strategies and knowledge that they need to integrate happiness and wellbeing into their curriculum and culture. Some carefully prepared videos and programmes dubbed 'Netflix for Wellbeing', focusing on staff, pupils, parents and community, have been made available to schools to embed positive attitudes inside the school and beyond.

Eton College has introduced classes on how to be grateful and kind, in an attempt to improve happiness among pupils. The college says education is not just about making people more employable. What matters is "educating the heart" to transform attitude so that pupils learn to treat classmates as collaborators rather than competitors.

Uz Azfal, a teacher in west London, has written an interesting book, *Mindfulness for Children*, drawing on inspiration from the practice of Buddhism. To make kindness fun for children-kindness ninja- they are encouraged to practice various acts of kindness in their home, community and school. The children are also taught practices such as 'Planet Apple' (looking deeply into an apple to understand the processes from the time it is picked and packed to being sold in the shop in order to help children understand the interconnectivity of things), 'Popcorn Party' (a practice where the children crouch into a ball like a kernel of popcorn to exemplify gratitude) and 'Brain Break' (where, three times a day, children stop whatever they are doing and focus on breathing). At a time when children are facing increasing stresses both in school and at home, Uz Azfal's book and teachings can be very helpful in establishing and promoting the connection between mindfulness and academic performance.

The prevailing culture of excessive long hours in schools has proved to be stressful to the wellbeing of both staff and students. Staff, particularly, are overburdened and not able to devote enough time to teaching. This has prompted some state schools to switch to a four-and-a-half day week in the belief that this will result in a much happier and productive form of teaching in schools. Many other schools are likely to shorten the school week to boost happiness.

In the USA, California has become the first state to delay the start of the school day to improve health and academic results. However, there is some opposition to this, on the ground that it would adversely affect working families who are unable to drop off their children later because of the nature of their work.

Happiness lectures by eminent Professor of Psychology Laurie Santos have become very popular courses at Yale University. One particular course, Psychology and the Good Life, is aimed at combating depression and anxiety among the students by teaching self-improvement strategies for behavioural changes through meditation, keeping 'gratitude' journals, acts of kindness, social links, exercise, sleep etc.

The appeal of this course has spread to many other university campuses. In the UK, the University of Bristol has initiated a course along the line of Professor Laurie's lectures that counts towards students qualifying for their degrees. This was introduced in response to the increasing concerns for students suffering from mental health problems. Psychologist Professor Bruce Hood, who runs a 12-week happiness course, explained it by saying, "Most people think that the path to happiness is success in jobs, salaries, material possessions and relationships. Ultimately, the aim is to give a greater understanding of what happiness is and how the human mind often sabotages it."

A UNICEF Report in 2013 found Dutch children to be the happiest in the developed world. Rina Mae Acosta, co-author of the book *The Happiest Kids in the World: Bringing up Children the Dutch Way* explained the reason by saying, "It's not that they (parents) allow everything, by any means, but everything is open to discussion" between Dutch teens and their parents. Furthermore, the work-life balance enables Dutch parents to share quality time with their children, rather than leaving them to do whatever they want to do on their own. In addition, there is also the awareness, on the part of the Dutch children, that no good will come from constantly comparing themselves with others regarding any kind of pursuit. 'Calm collaboration' is what they are taught through various mentoring programmes and this is what they try to practise in their daily life.

There are many lessons to be learnt here in the UK by going Dutch; particularly as the suicide rates are increasing among British teenagers because of loneliness, anxiety and depression.

Whilst improving happiness in schools is receiving due recognition, a way of combating depression amongst teenagers in Britain was recommended in a report published by the National Literary Trust in September 2016. A survey of about 50,000 pupils aged 8-18 showed that the children with the greatest love of literacy, which includes reading and writing, not only have better school results, they also have the highest levels of mental wellbeing. 'The bookworms make the happiest children'. This is certainly a promising finding to infuse positivity in the lives of school children at a time when, according to the Young Minds charity, "We hear time and again from parents whose children are self-harming."

Sir Anthony Seldon, former master of Wellington College believes that the crisis in the mental health of teenagers needs to be addressed as a matter of extreme urgency. He believes that instead of anti-depressant medication, hospitalisation or talking therapy, they need lessons in kindness and how to be 'at peace'. He wants the Departments of Education and Health to take an approach along this line to solve mental health problems.

13

HAPPINESS IN FILMS

Watching films about happiness is an alternative way of exploring this concept, visually. Most of the films I refer to are feel-good ones to warm your heart, with stories of love, humour and friendship, but I have also found several which seek to portray some useful lessons on ways to find happiness:

HAPPINESS (1935)

This is an irony-ridden Soviet film from the silent era, which begins with the philosophical question: "What is happiness and how we can achieve it?" Is it power, social status, wealth or something else?

The story revolves round the plight of a Soviet farmer to improve his material condition. A hapless loser, he comes across greed and the vested interest of people in different strata of society. As a result, he undergoes several misadventures but eventually finds some solace in being looked after by a totalitarian state. Sadly, this turns out to be a form of collectivised happiness that does not improve his individual wellbeing.

SHORTCUT TO HAPPINESS (2003)

Set in New York, this is the story of an ambitious but unsuccessful writer who is not able to sell his novels. Out of desperation, he sells his soul to the devil in exchange for fame and fortune. However, after getting what he wants – a book deal, money and women – he realises that he has lost love, friendship and the trust of people around him. He wants to get his soul back but is unsuccessful and, so, his life remains unfulfilled. He wants, but does not get, a second chance to appreciate and enjoy the good things he had before.

THE PURSUIT OF HAPPYNESS (2006)

This is an American biographical film about the life of an entrepreneur and his son. They face a continuous struggle after becoming homeless. The businessman manages to overcome this through hard work, determination and by establishing a strong father-son bond.

The film shows that the 'American Dream' of success and happiness can be a reality if one works hard for it, but there will always be several obstacles. The unusual spelling of the film's title comes from an incorrectly spelt mural on a wall.

HAPPY (2011)

Exploring different countries around the world, the film embarks on a journey from the swamps of Louisiana to the slums of Kolkata in search of what really makes people happy.

The film was inspired by the finding that some of the poorer countries surpass the richer ones on the list of the happiest nations in the world. The compelling reason given is that happiness is not primarily about money, wealth or status. Happiest moments in life are related to doing things that are meaningful and enjoyable, with a focus on family, friends, and personal growth.

The film is in accord with the current research work on happiness in positive psychology.

HAPPINESS (2013)

This is a film set in Bhutan, renowned for the invention of the concept of Gross National Happiness. The film captures a nine-year-old boy's desire to acquire a TV set to make him happier. It then follows his journey of exploration of the new technology in the city, and the realisation that the trade-off between his innocence and modern technology is likely to result in him losing many simple and peaceful aspects of his own tradition and culture.

FINDING HAPPINESS (2014)

This is a film about finding inward happiness by living in a community with like-minded people.

Narrated by an investigating journalist, it shows how people can live in harmony, peace and cooperation, in a community of their making called 'Ananda', which means joy.

This message was reflected in the life of the Bruderhof; a pacifist community founded in Germany. Such communities have spread over many countries. In the UK, they are located in villages in Kent (Nonington,) and East Sussex (Robertsbridge) with followers who have renounced their material possessions in order to live a life of peace and tranquillity.

HECTOR AND THE SEARCH FOR HAPPINESS (2014)

This is a short comedy-drama in which a psychiatrist, disillusioned with his boring life, goes on a journey to find happiness. On this journey, he meets several interesting people, including a professor involved in research on happiness. The important lesson he learns from his meetings is that true happiness isn't just one emotion but many, affecting human lives at different times, and in different circumstances. So, there is no one-size-fits-all formula for happiness; it varies from person to person.

THE HAPPY (2016)

This is the story of a graphic designer, who despite his material success is not a happy person. So, he goes on a journey in quest of peace of mind. He experiments with meditation, talk therapy and prescription drugs and also finds himself 'recklessly happy' in love. However, none of this lasts long and sadness follows. He decides to revert to his old life after realising that the search for happiness might have given him some kind of joy in life, but that unhappiness followed. So, there is no point in being obsessed with happiness.

The film also highlights the fact that there are different kinds of happiness: a) short-term bliss b) mid-term, lasting for a few days and c) long-term, which can endure for life.

All in all, the aforementioned films show that, as an art form, films can play an important role in highlighting various key aspects associated with happiness. There is a need for more happy films that can trigger new interest, inspire more research and promote useful discussion on paths to happiness.

14

SOCIAL MEDIA AND HAPPINESS

The links between social media and happiness are more complicated than is generally assumed. This is because social media can have both positive and negative effects on life satisfaction. However, there is a growing concern that our reliance on social media is having a detrimental effect on mental health, with the average person using their phones as much as 28 times a day.

In a survey in 2018 by CHILDWISE, a specialist research group, a substantial number of girls interviewed blamed social media for a rise in unhappiness, compared to a decade ago. Most were experiencing stress-related mental health problems.

An important study by the Institute of Social and Economic Research at the University College London and Essex University explored the happiness levels of both boys and girls using social media. Their report showed that both genders were suffering from emotional and social problems, but the teenage girls were experiencing them more acutely because of their tendency to compare themselves to others on Facebook, Instagram and other media. Apple created a 'beauty filter' app in their advanced phones XS and XS Max, to make people look more attractive than they are in real life. A 'constant flow of edited lives' in different forms of social media is effectively distorting the true image of the younger generation and their self-esteem. There is also evidence to show that the obsessive checking of mobile phones due to anxious minds before bed contributes to the lack of required hours of sleep as well as affecting general health.

A recent survey (2018) by Manchester, Brunel and Exeter Universities for the BBC found a very high rate of loneliness (40%) among the young Facebook generation (aged 16 to 24) compared with all adults (aged 65 to 75). *The Circle*, a reality TV programme shown on Channel 4, is quoted as an example for trivialising the way social media undermines people. Contestants, living in the same house, were only allowed to communicate online, without any face to face meetings. According to this BBC survey "Having a lot of friends on social media is no substitute for real companions'.

Ofcom, the UK's communication regulator, found that in 2018/19, around one in four people have been harmed by the online world through cyber-bullying and harassment. An important finding by the Happiness Research Institute in Copenhagen stressed that giving up Facebook boosts happiness by reducing anger and loneliness and increasing 'real world social activity'.

However, not all social media interactions are considered harmful. Social media can be great for looking back fondly on sweet memories. It is incredible how much information is readily available on the internet. "Use the internet every day" urged two economists from Norway, Fulvio Castelleci and Henrik Schwabe. They believe that it saves time and stress, provides access to information and helps to increase subjective wellbeing over the lifecycle. No doubt the internet has now become an invaluable supportive tool for day to day living.

Many others claim that social media has made teenagers more responsible and confident than their parents' generation. With many universities now gradually discarding fresher's weeks due to the risk of new students being subjected to coercion, humiliation and bullying, students are opting for online media as a better way of choosing clubs, making friends etc.

There are other proponents who say that a targeted downward social comparison on Facebook can boost happiness and life satisfaction. They do not believe that blaming social media platforms such as Facebook, Twitter and YouTube is the right solution to tackle associated problems. Their suggestion is both to guide and regulate the media better. In regards to banning the use of mobile phones or any other device, British political journalist Alice Thompson does not consider this the right way. This "isn't the solution: it's working out how to use devices for gain not pain and how to set boundaries for users and providers," she said.

However, the important question here is how to regulate or guide social media and by whom this should be carried out. Parents would not, because their regular monitoring would be resented by their children. Schools would not, because that would be considered undue interference by the parents themselves. Big tech companies have always been urged to behave responsibly, but their inertia to act shows how far they would be willing to go.

A matter of considerable interest is that, in March 2018, more than a third of Generation Z, from a survey of 1000 individuals, quit social media as it was making them anxious, sad and depressed. Further, many teens and twenty-somethings are discarding Facebook and similar social media platforms, opting for social networks such as 'GitHub' (an open source network) or 'House Party' (a group video chat application). These are gaining increasing recognition because of their objective to revive 'talking'. The young people are not followers of networks like Facebook or Twitter but more like members of book clubs with a limited number of friends and/or family members.

So, social media can be good, but in practice, it is increasingly used in ways that are particularly harmful to the younger generation. This explains why, in Silicon Valley, the senior executives of big companies are now sending their children to tech-free schools out of fear that technology is stifling their children's creativity. It is time to make social media companies work hand in hand with the government and happiness experts to assess both the positive and negative impact of social media in our lives.

15

WAYS TO BE HAPPY

There is no simple way to attain real happiness in life. Numerous paths have been suggested, from ancient times to modern. To feel ever-happy, an individual will wish to follow his or her chosen path. However, a path chosen by one may or may not work for another. Bearing this in mind, my knowledge and understanding has identified the following prescribed paths to happiness; some profound and meaningful, others amusing and light-hearted.

1) SOME GENERAL PREDICTORS

There are some generally accepted notions about what individuals should do to be happy: earn more money, travel the world, lose weight, fall in love, get married, buy a house, give up work and help the community are some suggested ways. Paul Dolan, Professor of Behavioural Science at the London School of Economics, has described these notions as 'Social Narratives'. As people are expected to conform to them, they fall into a narrative trap for how we should or should not behave.

According to research by the Office for National Statistics, published in May 2019, the key to happiness is to stay in good health and 'eat, drink and be married'.

Good health, no doubt, has a strong association with happiness but the same cannot be said, categorically, about the strength of eating and drinking for creating permanent wellbeing, as they can be harmful as well.

A married life is cited and often stereotyped as the single best predictor of a happy life. Marriage has been a part of different cultures for thousands of years and, no doubt, provides some important elements such as love, companionship, commitment, trust, shared values, stable family life and others that contribute to a satisfying human existence. However, the changing family structure and gradual acceptance of alternatives to married life have resulted in a significant change in attitudes and perceptions towards marriage and happiness in modern times.

According to Matthew Parris, the idea that "being a couple is the only way to achieve happiness is a prejudice which needs to be challenged." He has termed it 'monophobia'. There are countless people in this world who will never marry, there are others married and separated, and widows or widowers whom, for a large part of their lives, will be alone but not necessarily lonely and miserable.

"If you are afraid of loneliness, don't marry," said Chekhov. "When a lifelong relationship begins, a door closes on many other healthy relationships".

Confucius made a cryptic remark about marriage: "If you want to be happy for a day, get drunk. If you want to be happy for three days, get married. If you want to be happy forever, cultivate a garden."

"Happiness doesn't mean being with a man," said the actress Emily Fox. To her, 'happily ever after' is a fantasy and she feels good in her own company.

More recently, British actress Emma Watson has rebranded the word 'single' to 'self-partnered' to emphasise that women without partners can have a healthier, happier life if society stops eulogising marriage as the only way of having a meaningful relationship.

Professor Paul Dolan's latest book, *Happy Ever After*, argues against society's pro-marriage advocacy, saying that this a narrative trap to form the myth of a perfect life. In his research, the correlation between marriage and happiness has been found weak, for both men and women.

A Michigan University study has revealed that single women are happier than single men. A reason for this is that husbands create an extra seven hours of housework each week for their wives. A similar study in Australia found that once couples begin their married life, the time spent on housework goes up for women and down for men, irrespective of their employment status!

This perhaps explains why so many immensely successful women, such as Jane Austin, Greta Garbo, Katherine Hepburn, Coco Chanel, Condoleezza Rice, Carol Vorderman and Oprah Winfrey, chose to remain single and happy.

2) "WORK? FINE. HOME? FINE. HEART? NO"

We spend so much of our time working and there are many benefits associated with work, like helping people to be assertive, creative, committed, social minded and contribute to society. But does work make people happy?

The World Happiness Report (2017) has done some analysis of the relationship between work and happiness. Their three important findings were:

- Not being able to work i.e. unemployment is harmful, in many ways to people's wellbeing. Unemployed people suffer from low status, lack of recognition, poor social relations and so on.
- White-collar workers, in general, are happier than people working in blue-collar jobs, because they suffer less from the negative feelings of worry and stress.
- Regarding job satisfaction, it is always difficult to find the right 'work-life' balance at a personal level.

In an interesting article, *Living the Dream,* journalist for *The Sunday Times,* Matt Rudd, described the plight of the so-called affluent 'working fathers' who have high-profile jobs, nice homes and good family lives. From the outside, we would expect them to be happy, but they are not. For them, success is a 'poisoned chalice'. " Work? Fine. Home? Fine. Heart? No". That's how Matt Rudd summed up their frame of mind and failure to balance work and life.

Further, the working day is becoming longer and longer; in some cases, leading to a gruelling 55-hour week. Mobile technology, like laptops and smart phones, which should make the life-work balance better, mean that users are never strictly away from work and are adding an extra hour or two to their working day while commuting.

In his book, *The Compass and the Radar: The Art of Building a Rewarding Career While Remaining True to Yourself,* Paolo Gallo, who was a director at the World Bank in Washington, mentioned the crisis he had undergone in his working life. He termed this 'German soldier syndrome' – "head down, keep marching – a fast track to burnout." Eventually, he gave up his job and found happiness in being able to reconnect with what was more meaningful in his life, like his family. A widely acclaimed book, *Happier Now*, by Nataly Kogan, co-founder of Happier, a leading wellness company, reflects that her 'career burnt out' in her early working life in America.

Research shows that a happy workplace contributes to the wellbeing of the employees. There are several tips for making people feel happy in their jobs, such as doing meaningful work, flexible hours, regular breaks and a social environment. While these are useful tools, the bottom line is that work can make people happy only when it is not just a necessity but a pleasure.

3) SOME PROVEN PATHS

According to some happiness experts, there are accepted, proven, spiritual and practical paths to claim the inner joy that lies within us.

These are as follows:

a) YOGA AND MEDITATION:

Yoga originated in ancient India over 5000 years ago. The word 'yoga' is derived from the verb 'yuj', meaning to unite and establish a state of harmony between body and mind. It is said that there are two important aspects of a person; lower and higher selves. The lower is made up of our body, ego, and other demands and needs of our day to day life. The higher self enriches the lower through the practice of yoga and meditation to acquire a quiet mind and everlasting perennial joy.

There are various steps in the practice of yoga, including postures and breathing exercises for turning the mind inward. Meditation ('dhyana') is an advanced stage of yoga to gain clarity of mind and prepare it to be fully at peace.

Meditation has taken various forms in the Western world. Mindfulness meditation is practised by many Hollywood stars to improve their personal resilience and feelings.

A recent example is the 'beeja' (seed) form of meditation; brainchild of meditation expert Will William. Over the past seven years, he has taught meditation to many celebrities suffering from insomnia and depression. Inspired by the ancient Vedic knowledge, he wrote a book, *The Effortless Mind*, to explain his form of meditation. "Meditation is a circuit breaker for all the negative loops we have developed over life," he says in his book.

A relaxation technique growing as an alternative to meditation is called TRE-short for tension and trauma-releasing exercises. This involves a series of shaking movements to release muscular tightness and tension caused by stress. This has become popular with people who find it difficult to stay calm while meditating.

In 2014, some military top brass and civilian personnel in the UK were given lessons on mindfulness awareness from the Action for Happiness and the Oxford Mindfulness Centre to improve their personal resilience at difficult times. Two organisations hosting these courses were Action for Happiness and the Oxford Mindfulness Centre. The Defence Academy in Shrivenham in Wiltshire offered a few one-day courses along a similar line.

These are, no doubt, bold new initiatives, but there are critics who say, "You cannot bring enemies to their senses by preaching them the usefulness of happiness lessons." An editorial in the Sunday Times published an anecdote on 2 February 2014: "in a faraway conflict, we should threaten the warring parties with happiness classes. That should bring them to their senses."

A study led by Professor of Psychology Richard Davidson from the University of Wisconsin-Madison established that meditating for a long period of time has the potential to change the brain and stimulate the ability to train oneself in happiness.

This belief was instrumental in turning Mathieu Ricard, a French biologist and writer, to become a monk and find himself labelled by his followers as 'the most content human on the planet'. His life as a practising Buddhist made him leave the scientific life for a contemplative one. His book, *Altruism, The Power of Compassion to Change Yourself and the World*, expresses his strong belief that altruism and compassion for others can make humans better people, along with making society a happier place.

In recent times, there has been an extraordinary growth in the mindfulness technology market. Examples are successful meditation apps like Headspace, Calm, the Oura ring and Muse, a brain-sensing headband worn in meditating, often described as a 'meditation assistant'.

Muse is supposed to stimulate relaxation using the sounds of birds or storms. However, use of such technology for meditation is frowned upon by many traditional experts on meditation. To quote the Vedic meditation teacher, Light Watkins: "No serious mediator meditates with an app."

b) ANDY COPE'S SMALL HABIT CHANGES

The author Andy Cope's book *Happiness: Your Route Map to Inner Joy* has advocated some 'small habit changes' in our lives to reap the benefit of wellbeing in 'compound interest'.

The changes discussed in his book include taking regular exercise, getting good sleep, healthy eating habits, being affectionate, full enjoyment of our happy times, going screen-less, and being grateful for things which could have gone wrong but did not. He firmly believes that if one can realistically follow these habits; there will be significant differences in levels of happiness.

c) MIRIAM AKHTAR'S 12 HAPPINESS HABITS

Miriam Akhtar, a leading positive psychology practitioner and author of several books, is one of the experts who contributed to *The World Book of Happiness*. Her recent book, *The Little Book of Happiness,* has transposed a mass of useful information on the science of happiness into a pocketbook that readers find easy to read. The book reveals 12 evidence-based happiness habits like expressing gratitude, valuing kindness and practising mindfulness that will guide people to a fulfilling happiness. There is much in this book to change one's life for the better.

d) 15 MINUTES TO HAPPINESS

Author, podcaster and physiotherapist Richard Nichols has discovered an easy way to help people with happiness and wellbeing. His book, *15 Minutes to Happiness*, is a collection of exercises requiring only a few minutes each day. In his own words, they "can inspire you to take action that helps you to become a happier you." Each exercise is practised with scientific understanding and they have titles such as, 'Think Happy, Be Happy', 'Can You Buy Happiness?', 'Loving You is Easy' and 'Happy Body, Happy Mind'. The titles are closely aligned with the positive psychology movement.

e) MINDFULNESS AND MONEY MANAGEMENT

After the financial upheaval of 2008, a new group of managers and investors started offering investment planning along Buddhist and Indian practices of yoga and meditation. The idea was to impart calmness in the face of the various vicissitudes of the financial markets. George Kinder, a certified financial planner, has published a book, *The Seven Stages of Money Maturity*, with advice to use Buddhist ideas of patience and generosity for money management.

These financial gurus advocate the mixing of Eastern mysticism with money management. The aim of these proponents is as much to seek inner peace as to make big profits.

4) A FEW LOCALISED PATHS:

a) HYGGE – DENMARK:

Denmark is considered to be one of the most contented nations in the world. One reason for this is its embracing of a heart-warming concept called 'hygge' (pronounced 'hoo-ga') which means wellbeing. The term reflects an entire attitude to life of having a relaxed, cosy time with friends and family which is considered good for the soul. So, 'hygge' could be getting together for a meal over candlelight, meeting for coffee or beer, time spent with family or even on your own, with a good book in your hand. The important thing is not to leave an empty space around yourself and to create an ambience that helps you forget life's worries.

Other countries have similar expressions of 'cosiness of soul' but 'hygge' is so crucial to living a Danish way of life that the Danes consider it unique.

Some colleges in the UK have started teaching 'hygge' to students and it is also being exported to restaurants and bars in the form of decor, comfort, food and intimate settings in many countries. However, it would be wrong to assume that everyone in Denmark is happy. It is heartbreaking to be unhappy in a mostly happy society; the reason why the Danes have a very high suicide rate.

b) JAPANESE IKIGAI

If one aims for a longer, less stressful, healthier and pleasant and purposeful life, there is the new lifestyle Japanese mantra of 'ikigai'. It originates from the Japanese words 'iki' (to live) and 'gai' (reason). It involves doing small, spontaneous activities like drinking green tea, running 5km every morning, or any other pursuit, going against the Western notion of having one overarching purpose or goal, like a specific career, as a target. According to Ken Mogi, a Japanese neuroscientist and author of *The Little Book of Ikigai*, some simple pursuits help to build a happy and active life.

His book provided the middle-class guide to enlightenment, specifying the issues which take over our lives and make us unnecessarily stressed and unhappy.

It is worth stating some of these issues for their impact on the way we live our daily lives and how they should be tackled for a longer life, better health and greater happiness.

For example, it is not reasonable to stress about your child's school or tutor (not ikigai). Instead, help your child with a homework project (ikigai). Another example is not to worry about losing half a stone (not ikigai) but enjoy the fresh air and sights while walking or cycling (ikigai).

The underlying, simple message is to appreciate what you have in life, because that is more important than the fear of missing out.

5) PATHS (YOGA) GOING VIRAL

The yoga practice traditionally requires both an intellectual understanding of it and a high degree of dedication. Sadly, many people teaching and practising yoga and meditation nowadays appear to be living in a world of fantasy. The subtleties of yoga are being replaced by some unorthodox ideas *of* turning and twisting the body. As a result, we have yoga with dogs ('doga'), ponies, bunnies and goats, disco yogis, heavy metal yoga, chair yoga, sex yoga and many other self-promoted techniques.

Very recently, a luxury hotel in Keswick was offering yoga with lemurs. The hotel website said that doing yoga with lemurs 'heightens the sense of wellbeing for both lemur and human.' In health-fixated America, you are likely to get many of these 'wellness bender yoga sessions'.

Another new wellness trend is Gymbox in East London. This offers a fun class called Sexhale, described as fast-paced yoga sequences with a lot of deep breathing, stamping, and limb shaking and shouting with dance music.

Working out in the woods is another suggested way to boost calmness. There is a social enterprise called Primal Roots, in Kent, whose chosen method of being with nature is doing a handstand against a tree. According to this organisation, physiologically, the abdominal muscles, spine, digestion and balance are all boosted by being upside down. Being in touch with nature has, no doubt, an enormous amount of calming influence on our minds, but doing a handstand against a tree, in my opinion, can cause some physical harm.

More recently, Shaman Durek, an American, self-styled guru, rose to fame by marrying Princess Martha Louise of Norway. He is seeking to become the bridge between the spiritual and physical planes, advocating 'shamanism' to bring happiness into his clients' lives. His book, *Spirit Hacking: Shamanic Keys to Reclaim Your Personal power, Transform Yourself and Light Up the World,* is about what he calls 'consciousness rising'. This involves tapping into an individual's personal strength and empowering him or her with a higher form of positivity. However, Durek appears to be more in the limelight because of his relationship with the Norwegian princess and his close friendship with the actress Gwyneth Paltrow!

It should come as no surprise that there are many critics to these various forms of yoga experiments. According to them there is the 'traditional' yoga and there are the uncustomary versions. The uncustomary versions can never last long. The fall from grace of the teacher of hot yoga, Bikram Chaudhury, who, at one time, had millions of devotees, speaks for itself. Sadly, we are living in a world in which there is a craving for easy spiritual fixes and many people are taking advantage of this and making millions by mixing an age-old tradition with some new age hoo-ha.

16

CONCLUSION

It would be futile to pretend that it is going to be easy for me to sum up what I have set out in this book. It covers many different aspects and areas; none of which I can claim to be an expert in.

Professor of Psychology at Yale University, Laurie Santos, was once asked, "What's the future of happiness? Will there be a cure?" Her reply was, "The cure is a better understanding of what promotes wellbeing." This book aims to do that by offering a personal insight and introspection into various paths designed to make the individual a happier person.

The ancient philosophical concept of happiness is often described as a 'top down' approach and a by-product of virtue. The religious approach is considered prescriptive and tied to faiths in scriptures. Both seek to teach people how they ought to live, which is the reason why many modern happiness experts view these approaches as outdated in the modern world. The view that they are outdated is not sustainable, because the father of positive psychology, Martin Seligman, himself appears to have deviated from his earlier pragmatic approach of nurturing 'character strengths' as the only goal of happiness. He leaned towards supporting moral action as more relevant for human wellbeing. In his second book, *Flourish*, he emphasised the importance of six virtues – wisdom, courage, justice, humility, temperance and transcendence – for happiness. This change of emphasis reflects the importance he attached to ethics and spiritual connection. In the same book, Seligman wrote, 'Positive psychology called to me just as the burning bush called to Moses'. To his many critics, this sounded a lot like religion!

In spite of some justifiable criticisms, the sea change in the discipline of psychology, pioneered by Martin Seligman, has captivated innumerable happiness experts with its wellbeing promises. This has resulted in the creation of new vocabulary such as mindfulness, empowerment etc. in order to be happy. Further, this has given leisure service providers the opportunity to play the role of 'engineers' of leisure experience by combining some proven wellbeing-related factors like good health, family and close social relationships with some questionable, unconventional forms of finding happiness. As a result, people are being asked to learn how to live a happy life but they are also being induced into thinking, by several providers, that they are experiencing happiness, no matter how bizarre the chosen methods are, or the outcomes.

In previous chapters, I have mentioned several ideas and practices that have been prescribed by experts, coaches, counsellors and therapists to help people live life with joy and happiness. Some are universally tried and tested, like yoga and meditation – the scientific evidence lends enough support for these to remain lasting tools to many for a fulfilling life. Various studies have shown that listening to music boosts calmness; walking in the woods reduces health problems; group exercise improves quality of life; chair yoga enhances general wellbeing; gratitude and kindness foster joy, to give a few examples. The indigenous ones, like the Danish 'hygge' and Japanese 'ikigai', have much to teach us in regards to achieving a longer, less stressful and pleasant life. For people who lead a busy life, a quick fix, 15 minutes of daily exercise can help improve their wellbeing. As regards the newly emerging unusual and, in many cases, bizarre ideas and practices to seek happiness, such as yoga with dogs, Gong baths, Chakra balancing, handstands against trees, etc. it is my opinion that these will remain popular for a short time but are likely to fade when people no longer find them truly beneficial.

An eminent spiritual master, Swami Rama, said, "You are a creation of God, but happiness is your creation." This appears to suggest that it is our choice to be happy or unhappy, and that to be happy, you need to understand the meaning and purpose of life through your thoughts, speech and actions. His thinking is very much in line with what many other ancient and modern thinkers view as happiness. It also reflects my own mindset, associated with my personal experience in life which, in many ways, has influenced my understanding of what happiness is.

Like most people, I have been through various stages of happiness in my life. As a child, I enjoyed a very stress-free life as the son of a dutiful father and loving family. Then adolescence brought with it the stressful challenges of moving out of the family household, gaining higher education, making career choices, etc. This was followed by improving levels of happiness in middle age, which included arriving in this country, getting married, having children. My happiness level peaked after retirement, following the transition from a work-focused lifestyle to one with more opportunities for social interaction and thoroughly enjoyable leisure activities. So, in my case, happiness was not strictly the 'U-shaped curve' as suggested by the Dutch economist, Bert Van Landeghem, according to whom people are happiest at 25 and 65 and most miserable at 45. I am content with the way things turned out for me.

During my progression from childhood to what I am now – an octogenarian – I have learnt and acted on one very important lesson, which has stood me in good stead throughout my life. The lesson is what the eminent British Positive Psychologist Robert Biswas-Dieners said: "imagine life as a narrative that unfolds like a book with yourself as the author... making small edits that improve the story of your life and increase your happiness."

In my experience, the answer to the question, "What makes us happy?" has certain essential and important elements, which are:

1) HAPPINESS IN DIFFERENT FORMS:

There is no single, universally accepted path to happiness. People achieve fulfilment in different ways. Some find joy in mundane things like material values, work and family life; some through artistic pursuits, like art and music.

Many go to temples, churches, mosques or synagogues in search of spiritual uplifting. Some seek to find inner happiness in outlets for calm relaxations, such as yoga and meditation.

However, our happiness from relentless pursuit of hedonic type of pleasures and emotions fade away as we go about our everyday life. This means that, for happiness to last, we will need to focus inwards, towards the realisation of a fulfilling, long-lasting, tranquil state of mind. Being blessed by God; union with "Ultimate Reality" ('Atman'); submission to Allah; liberation from worldly attachments; yoga and meditation are some of the well-known spiritual and philosophical paths prescribed to reach this higher state of mind.

2) HAPPINESS IS NOT ALWAYS LOFTY:

Not everyone can attain this tranquil state of mind, but as the Islamic theologian Abu Hamid Ghazli said, we should at least endeavour to follow the path of those who attain this – wise men – to the degree we can emulate them. However, happiness does not need to be always abstract or lofty. There are many ways of seeking happiness and making ordinary life beautiful. To many individuals, the smallest things, like watching a bird fly, a flower bloom, listening to a nice piece of music, appreciating the beauty inherent in nature, are no less significant, in terms of happiness, than spiritual pursuits. The more one can experience those precious moments, the more he or she is likely to have a relatively contented life. As the Chinese proverb goes, 'the journey of a thousand miles starts with a single step'.

3) HAPPINESS OF 'JUST ENOUGH':

There are many ways of looking at happiness, but the one I found different to others and which resonates with my own thoughts, comes from Professor Paul Dolan. According to him, only by freeing ourselves from the myth of the perfect life, we might find a life worth living. This myth arises out of the prevailing assumption that more happiness can be achieved by living up to social narratives (as described in chapter 15) of ever more money and ever more markers of success in society (social expectations). These are traps of misery and failure because the aim for ever-increasing narratives generates ever-decreasing happiness in the long run, said Professor Dolan. His advice in his two books, *Happiness by Design* and *Happy Ever After*, is to move away from the standard definition of happiness to one of 'just enough' in contrast to the concept of "maximizing" in economics. He believes strongly that once you adopt this approach, it will stop you constantly worrying about striving for more and, so will have a positive impact on your happiness.

Professor Dolan's assertion appears to be an endorsement of moderation – balance and harmony – recognised as wise and apposite as a principle of life. We certainly do not always need much to be happy and content..

4) HAPPINESS AND EXTERNAL CIRCUMSTANCES:

At the heart of the positive psychology movement is the notion that external conditions and circumstances have no overarching influence over the bringing of joy into our lives.

Psychologist, Doctor Sonja Lyubomirsky, created a pie chart which shows the relative influence of different factors on our happiness: 50% reflects genetic influence, 40% is our power to change and only 10% is the effect of life circumstances. It is, realistically, difficult to accept this, and disregard the influence of factors such as age, sex, race, status, health, social relationships and the natural environment. All of these have positive and negative effects on our wellbeing. Doctor Lyubomirsky's claim that circumstances matter no more than 10% is considered a gross underestimation by her critics.

It is now universally acknowledged that social relationships, love, trust, family, friendships and concern for others give more satisfaction to human lives than material possessions, in the long run. This is backed up by the Mexican scholar, Leon R Garduno, urging everyone to "Look at life as a pie, divided into several different slices. Each slice represents one area or domain of importance in your life: family, friends, job, and inner life." His advice is to consider the relative importance of each slice and lead life accordingly. This has found support in London-based psychologist Sara Waite's Wheel of Life, derived from the Buddhist theory of balance. The idea is the same; dividing a circle into segments reflecting the different areas of life one wants to assess.

5) HAPPINESS AND NEO-OPTIMISM:

Positive psychology movement firmly believe that being an optimist plays an important part in making people happy. The dogma is that 'only positivity is the right way to live your life'. "Positive thinking has turned happiness into a duty and a burden," said Danish Psychologist Svend Brinkmann. What has got lost in this pressurized positivity culture, is the fact that life is wonderful from time to time but is also often tragic. To alienate people from normal, negative feelings and imply that unhappy people are to blame for their own misfortune has a detrimental effect on our emotional agility in facing different situations. There is also another important qualification to bear in mind; one cannot control everything. To seek happiness, it is always helpful to remember the American theologian Reinhold Niebuhr's famous *Serenity Prayer*:

'Grant me the serenity to accept the things I cannot change,
The courage to change the things I can,
And wisdom to know the difference'.

6) HAPPINESS AND VIRTUE:

An issue closely related to happiness is its relationship with virtue. Does a fulfilling life embrace both happiness and cultivation of one's virtues? Ancient philosophers like Aristotle believed that to achieve happiness, one needs to lead a commendable life. Stoic philosopher Cicero believed in the affinity between happiness and virtue. In the modern era, happiness is not viewed in the prescriptive sense of a value judgement. It is a subjective sense of satisfaction and wellbeing with one's life – more about *feeling* good rather than *being* good. However, positive psychology advocates such as Martin Seligman accepted that virtues such as calmness, resilience, wisdom, strengths are necessary attributes for our wellbeing and happiness. This echoes views that many ancient and modern thinkers have expressed over the years – that the path to true happiness embraces virtue.

7) HAPPINESS AND THE NATURAL WORLD:

That the human-natural world relationship has an impact on people's wellbeing has been recognised through the ages. It is said that, in the way nature works, there is a wisdom that is both profound and widespread. Stoic thinkers defined the goal of life as being in agreement with nature. The Chinese philosopher Zhuangzi referred to a mysterious intuitive power, 'Dao', present in our natural surroundings.

Humans enjoy the wonders of the natural environment and find peace and contentment in its presence. Nature connects us to each other and to the outer, larger world. There are the aesthetic benefits of nature as well as the spiritual and emotional ones. The English environmentalist poet, William Blake, echoed this feeling by saying, "The tree which moves some to tears of joy are in the eyes of others only a green thing... But to the eyes of many of imagination, nature is imagination itself".

Some of our happiest moments in life are when we are submerged in nature. It is no wonder that a large amount of research has stressed the positive impact of nature on our personal and social wellbeing.

SUMMING-UP:

Before concluding, it is worth quoting the commendable advice from the Mexican scholar, Jose de Jesus Garci Vega, about how our fleeting presence as individuals could have a lasting impact on the happiness of others in this world. He said, "To me, life is like a great party to which we all have been invited. Our only task is to enjoy it and be happy and make ourselves and others happy.... and to leave the room in the same condition as we found it or perhaps even better." I wholeheartedly agree with his advice to incorporate happiness into our daily lives.

The aforementioned seven essential elements, taken together, have three proven foundations of a happy and contented life: the self, bringing joy into other people's lives and the beauty of all that is around us. Happiness lies in exploring each of these elements to flourish bearing in mind that they have always been at the heart of various practices and paths to help people live life joyfully.

The self is the originator of all happiness and prospers towards a higher purpose and goal by going through different stages of living a virtuous and meaningful life. Aristotle asserted, long ago, that "man is by nature a social animal" – good social relationships are the most consistent predictor of a happy life. Doing good things for others helps the recipient, but it also has a beneficial effect on the mental and physical wellbeing of the doer. Humans are part of the natural world – they should learn to enjoy the wonders of the natural environment to find peace and contentment in its presence.

Happiness is the joyful experience of living in this beautiful world and enjoying every minute of it with fellow human beings and in communion with nature. Happiness is, certainly, more than 'a cigar called Hamlet'.

REFERENCES

Chapter 1: Introduction

'Less is More', *The Times*, 8 October 2019

'The search for happiness is all Greek to me', Oliver Moody, *The Times*, 6 February 2016

Chapter 2: Meaning of Happiness

'The Happiness of Excellence', Brianna West, 6 July 2016, https://medium.com›the-happiness

Chapter 3: Happiness History

'Aristotle and Happiness', www.pursuit-of-happiness.org

'9 of Greatest Philosophers Reveal the Secret to Happiness', Mike Nudelman and Chris Weller, *Independent*, 12 January 2017

'Stoicism: 101: An Introduction to Stoicism', www.holstee.com

15 October 2019

Chapter 4: Happiness in Different Religions

'Judaism and Happiness', Heshy Friedman, *Image Magazine*, 13 December 2007

'World Scripture – Joy and Happiness', www.unification.

net 2 April 2010 'Ananda, the State of Bliss or Happiness', Jayaram V, www.Hinduwebsite.com>anand

'What Happiness Is', '"Wüstenlicht" Orthodoxie-Orthodoxy', Archbishop Nathanial, 11 April 2007

'Happiness: Ancient and Modern Concepts of Happiness' A talk by Peter Kreeft 15 January 2014, Catholic Education Foundation.org,

'Does Guru Granth Sahib Describe Depression?', Kamaladeep Bhui and Dinesh Bhugra, *Indian Journal of Psychology*, January 2014

'*How to Remain Ever Happy*', M K Gupta, 2015

'*The Elements of World Religions*', Liz Flower, 1997

'Pew Research on happy Africans story is much more complex than we thought' Abdi Latif Dahir, 9 January 2018, www.journalism.org/news-author/abdi-latif-dahir

Chapter 5: Positive Psychology and *The World Book of Happiness*

'Why we should think critically about positive psychology in our universities' Carl Cederstrom, *The Guardian*, 7 February 2017

The World Book of Happiness, Leon Borman, 2010

'Is positive psychology all it's cracked up to be?' Joseph Smith, *The Highlight*, 27 November 2019

Chapter 6: Cynics of Happiness

'*Why I am happy to stay sad?*', Tim Lott, The Times, 26 November 2010

'Emilia Fox: Happiness doesn't mean being with a man' Michael Odell, *The Times*, 23 December 2017

'Happiness? No, give me the misery of devotion,' Philip Collins, *The Times*, 27 July 2012

'I was just as happy when I was a singleton,' Matthew Parris, *The Times*, 23 December 2017

Chapter 7: Growth Fetish – Money Does Not Buy Happiness

'Happiness is... not being obsessed by economic growth', Anthony Hilton, *Evening Standard*, 30 May 2013

'My handbags won't make you happy', Valentine Low, *The Times*, 1 November 2016

'Bad luck, your rich neighbour really is happier than you', Josh Glancy, *The Sunday Times*, 5 March 2013

'All the best things in life are (nearly) free', Libby Purves, *The Times*, 2 December 2013

'Economic growth may not buy happiness but it's a useful barometer', Oliver Kamm, *The Times*, 9 April 2018

'Economists say more income does not mean more happiness', *Texas A&M News Archives*, 10 January 2006

'Happiness is always £1 million away', Kaya Burgess, *The Times*, 6 December 2018

Chapter 8: Government and Happiness

'Win People's hearts and you'll come up trumps', Rachel Sylvester, *The Times*, May 3 2011

'Probably the world's happiest man', Nick Curtis, *The Times*, 6 September 2016

'Citizens Arise', Steve Hilton, *The Times*, 17 May 2015

Chapter 9: Happiness in the UK

'Does money really make us happy?' Nigel Kendall, Channel 5 Survey Result, 1 January 2017

Survey of the Office for National Statistics on Happiness Levels, 2019

'Take me to your guru: one man's quest to join the wellness movement', Michael Odell, *The Times*, July 24 2018

'The life coach to the uber-rich (Michael Serwa) confesses all', Robert Crampton, *The Times Magazine*, 9 February 2019

'Britons getting richer... but not any happier', Greg Hurst, *The Times*, 5 February 2019

'Could being British hold the secret to long-term happiness?', Judith Woods, *The Telegraph Lifestyle,* 3 April 2018

'Kate's forest bathing, Harry's meditating – wellness is a right royal fad', Hannah Jane Parkinson, *The Guardian*, 16 January 2019

'Prince Charles funds yoga and meditation for young prisoners', Hannah Furness, *The Telegraph*, 8 January 2019

'Keep calm and meditate like Prince Harry', Helen Rumbelow, *The Times*, 16 January 2010

'Phew! It's a long slog, this happiness lark', Roland White, *The Sunday Times*, 17 April 2011

'Age of Empire gave Britain something to smile about', Rhys Blakely, *The Times*, 15 October 2019

Chapter 10: Happiness in America

'Wealthy have ruined Burning Man festival', Ben Hoyle, *The Times*, 14 February 2019

'Eat Pray Sing', Sanjiv Bhattacharya, *The Sunday Times*, 12 August 2018

World Happiness Report: 'Americans are unhappiest in years', Alex Ward, *Vox*, 21 March 2019

'Americans are becoming less happy and there's research to prove it', Christopher Ingraham, *Washington Post*, 23 March 2018

'Here's How Happy Americans Are Right Now', Alexandra Sifferlin, The Harris Poll, time.com

'The Happiness of Pursuit', Jeffrey Kluger, Time July 8 2013 content.time.com.

'Free to Be Happy', Jon Mecham, *Time*, nation.time.com/2013/06/27/free-to-be-happy, 27 June 2013

Chapter 11: Happiness in India

'What we can learn from the definition of happiness in India', Alissa 18 February 2018 http://happinessaroundtheglobe.com/happiness-in-india

'Happiness in India and the West', Diederik Mallien, www.diegomallien.com/travelling-and-culture/happiness-india-west-2, 31 March 2017

Song of India: Tales of Travel and Transformation, Mariellen Ward, 2010

'The great Indian happiness tragedy', Thomas Sajan,

www.thehindubusinessline.com/opinion/the-great-indian-happiness-tragedy-ep/article23384587.ece, 29 March 2018

'Happiness in India' from book *Happiness across cultures, views of happiness and quality of life in non-western countries'*, Robert Biswas-Diener, Louis Tay and Ed Diener 1st ed 2012

An Uncertain Glory, Jean Dreze and Amartya Sen, 2013

'India to create a ministry of happiness', Andrew Marszal, *The Telegraph*, 1 July 2016

'Government Work – Could a Ministry of Happiness improve the lives of India's citizens?', Maddy Crowell, www.lapham squarterly.org/happiness/government-work, 27 July 2019

Chapter 12: Happiness in Schools and Colleges

'University to give students crash course in happiness' and 'Eton pupils given lessons in how to show gratitude', Nicola Woolcock, *The Times*, 11 May 2019

'Law? Coding? You'll never guess the most-wanted course at Yale', Miranda Bryant, *The Times*, 8 August 2018

'Children find their inner kindness ninja', Damien Arnold, *The Times*, 2 February 2019

'Head shortens school week to boost happiness', Rosemary Bennett and Nicola Woolcock, *The Times*, 27 February 2019

'Don't worry be happy, pupils in India told', Saptarshi Ray, *The Times*, 24 July 2018

'Cool, smart, independent, happy. Why are Dutch teens so sorted?', Mark Smith, *The Times Magazine*, 2 March 2019

Chapter 13: Happiness in Films

'Top 3 inspiring movies and documentaries about happiness- Art, Culture and Leisure' Arlo Laibowitz www.happiness.com

Chapter 14: Social Media and Happiness

'Children who love reading feel happier', Nicola Woolcock, *The Times*, 26 September 2018

'Parents should calm down about social media', Alice Thomson, *The Times*, 19 September 2018

'Social media blamed for rise in unhappiness among girls', Greg Hurst, *The Times*, 19 September 2018

'Silicon Valley's tech-free school is a hit', Tom Knowles, *The Times*, 10 November 2018

Chapter 15: Ways to Be Happy

'Review: Happy Ever After: Escaping the Myth of the Perfect Life by Paul Dolan–how to find happiness' Christina Patterson The *Sunday Times*, 13 January 2019

'Top brass put at ease with happiness class', Mark Hookham, *The Sunday Times*, 2 February 2014

'Single women lead a healthier, happier, longer life if only couples would let them enjoy it', Caroline Criado Perez, *The Sunday Times*, 10 November 2019

'Hygge: A heart-warming lesson from Denmark' Justin Parkinson, 2 October 2015 https://www.bbc.com/news/magazine-34345791

'Happiest man in the world offers app to enlightenment', Esther Addley, *The Guardian*, 30 May 2015

'The man who taught Tom Bradby to get a good night's sleep', Damien Whitworth, *The Times*, 25 April 2019

'Key to happiness? Eat, drink and be married', Greg Hurst, *The Times*, 16 May 2019

'Lemur yoga: Doga is over, now it's all about lemoga', Kate Wills, *The Times*, 25 April 2019

'People come for Utopia, but is that what they find?', Andrew Billen, *The Times*, 22 July 2010

'Financial gurus seek inner peace – and big profits', Will Pavia, *The Times*, 11 June 2013

'This woman can cure your foblo', Lucy Holden, *The Times*, 10 September 2018

'What do you think of my pose?', Robert Crampton, *The Times*, 6 March 2019

'Forget FOMO it's all about JOMO', Anna Maxted, *The Times,*13 April 2019

'I have had people say that I'm like Rasputin', Eve Barlow, *The Times*, 29 July 2019

'Move over Scandi! We want to live the ikigai life now', Rachel Carlyle, *The Times*, 12 August 2017

'Cool, smart, independent, happy. Why are Dutch teens so sorted?', Mark Smith, *The Times Magazine*, 2 March 2019

Happiness: Your Route Map to Inner Joy, Andy Cope, 2017

15 Minutes to Happiness, Richard Nicholls, 2017

'Andy Cope's 10 hacks for happiness and realistic resolutions in 2019', *The Irish News*, 3 January 2019

Happy Ever After, Paul Dolan, 2019

The Little Book of Happiness, Miriam Akhtar, 2019

'Living the Dream', Matt Rudd, *The Sunday Times Magazine*, 9 December 2018

Chapter 16: Conclusion

'Can this man make me happy?', Robert Crampton, *The Times Magazine*, 12 January 2019

'The hot yoga debate just got fiercer', Peta Bee, *The Times Body & Soul*, 19 November 2013

'The joy audit: how to have more fun in 2020', Elle Hunt, *The Guardian*, 1 January 2020

'Are you suffering from TOXIC positivity?', Fleur Britten, *The Sunday Times Style*, 1 December 2019

'Paulo Coelho: Writing in a Global Language', Alan Riding, *New York Times*, 30 August 2005

Happiness by Design, Paul Dolan, 2014

'*Happiness is your Creation*', Swami Rama, compiled by Pandit Rajmani Tigunait, 2005

About the Author

Sujit Bhattacharjee was born in India and has lived in the United Kingdom for over 52 years. Educated both in Kolkata and London, he holds Bachelors and Masters degrees in Political Science, Law and International Relations. After working across the British Civil Service for 35 years he retired from the Ministry of Defence in 2004. Since then, he is best known as a writer and speaker on various cultural and socio-political issues. He also has a long history of active involvement in various social, cultural and political organisations.

This is Sujit Bhattacharjee's second book. His first (titled *"My Journey from an Asian British to British Asian"*) was an autobiography of his life and experiences of living both in India and in the UK and an exploration of the view that one's identities can be both multiple and situational.

www.ingramcontent.com/pod-product-compliance
Lightning Source LLC
Chambersburg PA
CBHW051706040426
42446CB00008B/746